FAIRWORLD cookbook

Introduction by Sophie Grigson

**100 fabulous recipes using
FAIR TRADE ingredients**

TED SMART

Acknowledgements

The *Fair World Cookbook* was inspired by the work of Jo Rodgers and a group of Oxfam volunteers in the Highgate (London) Oxfam shop. Their enthusiasm for Oxfam's Fair Trade foods led her to collect together a range of recipes, many of which are included here. Our thanks to them and the many volunteers giving their time to support Oxfam.

Oxfam and Cassell would also like to say a special thank you to Sophie Grigson who has generously given of her time and recipes. Her enthusiastic and unstinting support has been an inspiration to everyone involved with the book. We are, too, extremely grateful to the celebrity chefs who took the time to send us recipes for the book. Their help has been invaluable. Finally, everyone at Oxfam and Cassell thanks James Fisher for pulling together the recipes on offer to make such a mouthwatering collection for us all to enjoy.

First published in the UK 1997 by Cassell, Wellington House, 125 Strand, London, WC2R 0BB

This edition produced for
The Book People Ltd,
Hall Wood Avenue,
Haydock,
St Helens WA11 9UL

Copyright © Oxfam Activities 1997

British Library Cataloguing-in-Publication Data
A catalogue record for this book is available from the British Library

ISBN 0–304–34944–5

A 10 per cent royalty on the sale of this book will be donated to Oxfam (United Kingdom and Ireland), a registered charity number 202918. This royalty will go towards Oxfam's Fair Trade work supporting food producer groups around the world. Oxfam (United Kingdom and Ireland) is a member of Oxfam International.

Designed by Dave Crook
Recipes compiled and tested by James Fisher
Photographs by Amanda Heywood
Food styling by Liz Cohen
Edited by Wendy Hobson

Typeset in Bembo & Helvetica
Printed and bound in Great Britain by Bath Press Colourbooks, Glasgow

Contents

Introduction

Many years ago, when I was a student, I suffered coffee from the Students' Union shop, bought somewhat reluctantly because I knew that it was the right thing to do. It tasted perfectly vile, but it was an early years Fair Trade product, and I knew that it benefited workers somewhere or other and that I should really sup up and shut up.

How times have changed. Now I buy Cafédirect coffee with enthusiasm because it tastes so good. It's a top-class offering, a pleasure to drink, and a tribute to its growers and producers. An increasing number of Fair Trade products, from the delicious Maya Gold chocolate to dried fruits and nuts, are sold in Oxfam's and many other shops. A stroke of luck for cooks, since the quality is always impeccable, and often exceptional.

Encoded within the fabric and contents of each jar and packet is a remarkable hidden story. The stories all begin with the same premise, that of fair trade. The Oxfam Fair Trade campaign is founded on the belief that all people have the basic right to earn a living and to live free from poverty. By cutting out middlemen and offering technical support, the Oxfam Fair Trade Company ensures that people are receiving a fair wage for their work and expertise, and that their products reach a wide market. Who could fail to applaud them for that? And yet it is only, perhaps, when we really begin to understand the enormous impact that the Fair Trade campaign can have on individual lives, that it takes on real meaning.

The kingdom of Swaziland, not much bigger than Wales, is tucked away neatly between South Africa and Mozambique. As the plane dips down below the cloud, the vista below is breathtaking. Gentle mountains fold up all around, strewn with boulders, but it is the greenness of the land, scarred here and there by the rich, fertile red earth of the roads and fields, that comes as the biggest surprise.

That first impression is one of relative prosperity and considerable beauty. On closer acquaintance, the pretty little homesteads that I'd glimpsed from the plane, with their round thatched huts, reveal a different story. Poverty is no stranger here. Polygamy is common, and many men will have several wives and numerous children. If they do find work, the money they earn will barely be enough to support one family, let alone all their dependent wives and children. The end result is that the women are the ones who scrape and struggle to bring in enough money to feed, clothe and educate their children. A meagre existence, blessed by remarkable, indomitable, sunny natures that rise above the meanness of the hand that life has dealt them.

Discreetly hidden away in Manzini, Swaziland's second city, is a small business that has transformed the lives of some of the country's poorest families. Eswatini Swazi Kitchen is a truly remarkable place, though at first glance it looks like so many other well-organized, well-run little enterprises. In the cool, clean, white-walled building, a team of women make some of the most delicious jams and chutneys you can lay your hands on (the latest Peach and Ginger Jam is a humdinger!).

Mildred Henwood is the manager, and one of the driving forces behind Eswatini's success. She is a heavenly, warm, straight-talking tornado of a woman, who leaves a wake of devoted friends and admirers wherever she goes. Thirteen women are employed here full time, with a team of frequently employed occasional workers called in to deal with gluts of fruit and vegetables, or the demands of a large order.

The 'factory' atmosphere is bright and happy; the women chat and laugh and sing as they work; the air is scented with the perfume of ripe fruit and sugar and spices. For them, Eswatini (which, incidentally, means Made in Swaziland) has been a lifeline. Many, when they first came to Eswatini, were convinced that they were worthless and that they had no future. It's hard to believe that when you meet them now.

When Ngotula, a mountain woman and single mother of three, first came to the building she was terrified of electricity and didn't want to return if the lights were on. Now she is in charge of all electrical machines, and can tell when the freezers are labouring or if a bearing is going. Allainh is the cook in charge of sauces and chutneys, but when she started work she didn't even know how to count. Now she is perfectly at home with the ins and outs of testing the pH of her chutneys and has no difficulty wielding a refractometer as she tests for sugar content. Lomi was disabled and missed much of her schooling. Now she is in charge of stock taking and invoices, is taking a course in computing, and is Mildred's right-hand woman on her forays to suppliers.

Many of the ingredients for their preserves are sourced from local farmers, who grow crops on the small plots of land granted to them by their chief. It often happens, in this fertile but impoverished land, that they have no transport, or cannot afford to employ people to harvest their crops. The gaily painted Eswatini van comes to the rescue, driven at break-neck speed along pot-holed, untarred roads, Mildred at the helm. 'We will slash the grass and pick crates of fruit and vegetables,' she says.

When I arrived in early April, they were cutting and slicing and cooking up the last of the year's mangoes, sweet and plump and oozing honeyed juices. Guava jam – thick, pulpy and fragrant – was simmering on the stoves, watched over and stirred from time to time by Lindiwe, manager of jam cooking. Mildred and Lomi took me to meet some of the women who gather the wild fruit when it is at its best.

The meeting place was a small homestead set back half a mile from the main road that bisects the country. In the shade of a tree, a baby lay asleep on a mat amidst a gaggle of chickens, a few young kids and a host of fat, hefty melons. Half a dozen women greeted Mildred and Lomi with huge smiles and gales of happy laughter. Mildred's regular visits ensure a small but reliable income for these women, whose only other source of income would be selling firewood and chickens from the side of the road.

Coco arrived with her four-month-old grandson, Final, swaddled on to her back. He gurgled contentedly on my lap for a while. The small sum of money that Coco and her daughter earn from supplying Eswatini Swazi Kitchen will ensure that this snuggling, trusting child is fed and clothed as he grows.

A day later, my heart was stolen again by another four-month-old, little Lindiwe. I met her mother amongst a grove of trees high up in the mountains, where she had come, along with some eighty or so other women, to sell her hand-made grass baskets to Eswatini for their gift-packs. Other children played amongst the tussocks of coarse grass and the boulders. Their education and their future, and that of pretty, laughing little Lindiwe, will be guaranteed by their mothers' neat fingers, and Eswatini's overseas trade.

Once a month, Mildred and Lomi set out to a run-down training centre a little way from the city. Yet another gathering place, this time for a group of eighteen physically handicapped men and women with glistening eyes, a rapier-sharp sense of humour, and skilled hands, some of whom have travelled over 90 kilometres to the rendezvous. They carve wooden spoons topped with miniature animals. At a price of one and a half emalangeni each (about 20p), these additions to the gift-packs allow them to buy their own wheelchairs and crutches in a country where the physically handicapped are rejected as too burdensome unless they can pay their own way.

The profits from Eswatini Swazi Kitchen do not make their way into the pocket of some fat cat. Far from it. They speed straight to the aid of four homes for street children. Boys, often as young as six or seven, whose families cannot support them or who are orphaned or unwanted, make their way to the larger towns, sleeping rough, stealing and shoplifting, and shivering in dark doorways. These spartan homes are a haven, though heaven knows, they lack all but the most basic amenities.

Since its beginnings some seven years ago as part of the Manzini Youth Care Project, Eswatini Swazi Kitchen has grown beyond everyone's hopes. It is a small business, yet it reaches out to transform the lives of several hundreds of people and their dependants. Though regular income is important, there is more to its remit than that. A sense of personal responsibility, of involvement, of pride is embedded in everyone's contribution, giving a quiet dignity to suppliers and employees.

What a story is encapsulated in those glass jars! And it is just one of many such stories, scattered across the world. The Fair Trade campaign ensures that poor people have a chance to work to improve their lives and those of their children, and it gives us the chance to thrill our tastebuds with their joyfully produced goods. Buying Fair Trade products has nothing to do with pity or charity. It is about good taste and good sense, it bestows dignity on the producer, and helps to create a Fairer World for us all.

Sophie Grigson

Snacks and Starters

Spiced fried dahl

Serves 4

> 250g (9 oz) yellow split peas, soaked overnight and drained
> 2 tablespoons ghee or clarified butter
> 1 small onion, finely chopped
> 3 garlic cloves, minced
> 2 teaspoons fresh root ginger, finely chopped
> 1 tablespoon curry paste
> ½ teaspoon Fair Trade ground turmeric
> 25g (1oz) Fair Trade sun-dried mango, very finely diced
> salt and Fair Trade ground black pepper
> plain flour for dusting
> 500ml (17fl oz) vegetable oil for deep-frying

This is a Sri Lankan starter called *masala wada* that combines hot and fruity flavours. All the balls should be served on one large plate in the middle of the table for everyone to help themselves using their hands. Serve with a bowl of yoghurt or lime pickle if you are a fan of sweet and sour tastes.

Method

Coarsely grind the soaked split peas (you can use a food processor). It does not need to be a smooth paste; having a few lumps to bite into is nice.

Heat the ghee or clarified butter in a pan. Add the onion, garlic and ginger and cook gently until they begin to soften. They do not need to be cooked right through. Add the curry paste and turmeric and keep turning the mixture around with a wooden spoon so that it does not stick. After 1–2 minutes you will begin to smell the aroma of the curry spices. Add the mango and season to taste with salt and pepper. Remove from the heat and leave to cool.

When the onion mix has cooled, stir it into the split pea purée. Shape the mixture into balls between 2 dessertspoons, then roll them and place them on a floured board. Heat the oil in a deep-fat fryer or large pan and fry the balls a few at a time for 1–2 minutes until crisp and golden. Serve hot.

Fair Trade

Mango slices are solar-dried in Burkina Faso, one of the world's poorest countries. The farmers are organized into co-operatives with a tradition of collective field work.

Spiced chickpea croquettes

Makes 8

225g (8oz) chickpeas, soaked overnight and drained

1 egg

2 tablespoons Fair Trade dried oregano

4 garlic cloves, crushed

juice of 2 lemons

1 teaspoon ground cumin

1 teaspoon Fair Trade dried basil

1 teaspoon Fair Trade ground turmeric

a small handful of chopped fresh coriander

a pinch of Fair Trade chilli powder

salt and Fair Trade ground black pepper

2 tablespoons plain flour

1 egg, beaten

50g (2oz) bran

vegetable oil for deep-frying

These croquettes are spicy and would be best served with a yoghurt and cucumber salad. As a starter, serve two croquettes for each person. The croquettes blacken very easily so keep a constant eye on them while you are cooking to prevent this from happening.

Method

Cook the chickpeas in simmering water for 1 hour or until tender, then drain and reserve the cooking liquor. Mash the chickpeas and blend with 3 tablespoons of the reserved cooking liquor, the herbs, spices, salt and pepper. Shape the mixture into 8 croquettes. Dust the croquettes lightly with flour, then dip them in the beaten egg and roll them in the bran. Heat the oil in a frying pan and fry the croquettes over a medium heat for 7–10 minutes until golden on all sides. Drain well and serve hot.

Korokoro

Serves 6

350g (12oz) plain flour
3 tablespoons Fair Trade golden caster sugar
½ teaspoon Fair Trade ground cinnamon
175ml (6fl oz) boiling water
extra plain flour and Fair Trade golden caster sugar for rolling
200ml (7fl oz) vegetable oil for deep-frying

This snack falls into the category of being a sweet treat. It is African in origin, as you might guess from the name, and is quick and easy to make. When rolling out the dough, try to make the rolls as long as possible so that you end up with a what looks like a bed of wriggling snakes on your plate.

Method

Mix the flour, sugar and cinnamon with the boiling water to make a soft but firm dough. Set aside and allow to cool.

Dust your hands with flour. Take a knob of dough and roll it between the palms of your hands to make sausage shapes about the thickness of a pencil. Try bending these into different shapes. Then roll the *korokoro* in the extra sugar. Heat the oil in a heavy-based frying pan and fry the shapes for about 1½ minutes until golden. Drain well and serve hot.

Fair Trade

'People's lives are improving now ... those who were very poor before can now buy blankets, and clothes for their wives and children.'

Lost bread

Serves 2

75g (3oz) butter
2 egg yolks
50ml (2fl oz) milk
2 teaspoons Fair Trade ground cinnamon
1 teaspoon salt
Fair Trade ground black pepper
4 slices of bread
a knob of butter for frying
1 tablespoon Fair Trade golden caster sugar

This is a recipe that comes from the depths of English annals and delights in the old name of *payn pur-dew* – taken, very loosely, from the French! With a stretch of the imagination you can see this as an Arthurian dish. It is sweet recipe which can be eaten at breakfast, as a mid–day snack or even as a late night binge.

Method

Clarify the butter by gently heating it in a pan until it separates into a liquid and sediment. Drain off the melted butter into a separate bowl, discarding the sediment. Whisk the butter into the egg yolks, then stir in the milk, cinnamon and salt and pepper. Dip the bread into the egg mix and let any excess egg drip off the bread before frying.

Melt a knob of butter in a frying pan and keep it hot. Fry the bread for 3 minutes on each side until crisp and golden. Remove the bread from the pan, sprinkle with sugar and eat while still hot.

Fair Trade

Fair Trade means that the people who actually grow and produce our food get a fair return for their work. 'I can buy food and medicine when I need it and I can afford to put my kids through school.'

Spinach and walnut omelette

Serves 6

2 leeks

150g (5oz) spinach

4–5 spring onions

6–8 eggs

2–3 tablespoons chopped fresh parsley

3 tablespoons chopped fresh mixed herbs

2 tablespoons Fair Trade walnuts

2 tablespoons Fair Trade raisins

salt and Fair Trade ground black pepper

2 tablespoons butter, softened

Claudia Roden has written several cookery books; this particular recipe, *kukuye sabsi*, comes from *New Book of Middle Eastern Food*. She describes this dish as being an oven-baked, Persian-flavoured omelette. Arab omelettes are not light and fluffy like their French counterparts, but are firm and more like an egg cake. The egg is not the filling but the binding agent. This omelette is bursting at the seams with the filling and can be cut like a cake. It can be served hot or cold, and makes a perfect lunch served with a selection of side dishes such as fresh olives, grated hard-boiled eggs, red onion salad dressed with olive oil and lemon juice, and a fresh mixed salad. Or it can be served simply with yoghurt as a side dish.

Method

Preheat the oven to 160°C/325°F/Gas 3 and butter an ovenproof dish. Wash all the vegetables, dry them and chop them very finely. Beat the eggs in a large bowl. Add the chopped vegetables, parsley and mixed herbs, walnuts and raisins. Season to taste with salt and pepper and mix well. Pour the egg mixture into the dish and cover with a lid or foil. Bake in the oven for 30 minutes, then remove the cover and continue to cook for a further 15 minutes until the vegetables are tender and the eggs are set with a golden crust on top.

Fair Trade

Buying Fair Trade products not only increases the incomes of poor farmers, it helps them to feel more secure about the future so that they can plan ahead.

South African kebabs

Serves 2-4

450g (1lb) lamb, cubed
2 garlic cloves, crushed
1 onion, finely chopped
1 teaspoon Fair Trade ground ginger
2 teaspoons ground coriander
salt and Fair Trade ground black pepper
5 lemon leaves or 1 teaspoon grated lemon zest
2 teaspoons Fair Trade golden caster sugar (optional)
50ml (2fl oz) milk

For the marinade
50ml (2fl oz) vinegar or tamarind water
1 teaspoon Fair Trade golden caster sugar
4 tablespoons curry powder
1 teaspoon Fair Trade ground turmeric
1 tablespoon Fair Trade guava extra jam
2 bay leaves
1 fresh chilli, deseeded and finely chopped

Spicy marinades, pungent pickles, sweet-and-sour chutneys and curries are some of the delights of South African food. But a bitter aftermath lingers – the memory of a coercive regime that predated apartheid. For these exotic tastes were brought to the Cape by Malay slaves imported from Indonesia in the seventeenth century by the ruling Dutch. The most prized slaves were the cooks who gingered up bland Dutch fare into something unforgettable. To make these *sasaties*, as they are called, the meat mixture should rest in the fridge for 4 hours before you put it into the marinade and the marinated meat should be left overnight.

Method

Place the cubed lamb in a deep bowl and mix in the garlic, onion, ginger, coriander, salt and pepper. Scatter the lemon leaves or zest and sugar, if using, on top, then pour on the milk. Place in the fridge for at least 4 hours.

To make the marinade, boil the vinegar or tamarind water with the sugar, curry powder, turmeric, guava jam and a little salt. Simmer for 5 minutes or until the sugar has dissolved. Allow to cool, then add the bay leaves and chilli, mixing well.

Drain the milk from the meat mixture. Place the meat in the bowl containing the marinade, stir it round so that all the ingredients mingle. Cover and leave overnight in the fridge.

To cook the kebabs, remove the meat from the marinade and thread on to skewers. Grill under a hot grill or on a barbecue for about 10 minutes, turning frequently until the meat is cooked through and tender. Heat the marinade to make a sauce to serve with the kebabs.

Fair Trade

The Fairtrade Mark shows that a product is 'people friendly'. When you see it, you know that you are choosing 'not for profit' alternative trading organizations like Oxfam's Fair Trade Company.

St John's Welsh rarebit

Serves 6

75g (3oz) butter
100g (4oz) plain flour
1 tablespoon mustard powder
1 teaspoon Fair Trade chilli powder
a pinch of salt and Fair Trade ground black pepper
120ml (4fl oz) Worcestershire sauce
250ml (8fl oz) Guinness or other stout
675g (1 ½ lb) Cheddar, grated
6 slices of bread, toasted

Savoury cheese dishes were a popular Victorian tea-time dish. It has become a recent trend to re-create old classic dishes and this one can be found on the menu at St John's restaurant in the City of London.

Method

Melt the butter in a pan over a low heat and stir in the flour and spices, salt and pepper. Pour in the Worcestershire sauce and Guinness. Mix in the cheese and whisk until you have a stiff, smooth paste. Do not allow the mixture to boil otherwise the cheese will separate. Turn out on to a tray and allow to cool and set. This may take up to 4 hours.

When the spread is set, divide it into 6 and spread over the toast. The rarebit is ready for grilling or it can be kept in the fridge for 2–3 days. To finish off the rarebit, just place under a hot grill, spread-side up, and toast for 2–3 minutes until the cheese bubbles and browns.

Slow-braised honey and cider pork

Serves 10–12

1.75kg (4lb) belly pork
1.75 litres (3 pints) water

For the marinade

1 teaspoon Fair Trade ground cinnamon
1/2 teaspoon Fair Trade chilli powder
1 teaspoon Fair Trade ground black pepper
1 teaspoon Szechuan peppercorns, crushed
2 tablespoons Fair Trade wild blossom honey
350ml (12fl oz) soy sauce
175ml (6fl oz) sweet cider
10 garlic cloves
5cm (2in) piece of fresh root ginger

As well as being an interesting starter, this makes an easy and very tasty family lunch dish.

Method

Mix together the cinnamon, chilli and peppers. Press this mixture down on both sides of the pork. Mix the remaining marinade ingredients and pour over the spiced belly. Place in the fridge and leave to marinate overnight.

Preheat the oven to 150°C/300°F/Gas 2. Choose a shallow roasting dish in which the pork will neatly fit but have space for the marinade. Pour in the water and all the marinade. Bring to the boil, then cover with foil and bake in the oven for 2½–3 hours. Turn and baste the pork every 30 minutes during cooking. Do not allow the meat to dry out. Just add a little more water if necessary. The pork is cooked when it gives no resistance to a metal skewer. Strain the liquor into a pan and simmer gently until it thickens to a syrup. Spoon the sauce over the meat and serve with boiled new potatoes and young spinach.

Chinese five-spice fried squid

Serves 4

- 250g (9oz) plain flour
- 3 tablespoons Chinese five-spice powder
- 2 tablespoons Fair Trade ground black pepper
- 2 tablespoons Fair Trade chilli powder
- 2 teaspoons salt
- 450g (1lb) squid, gutted and skinned
- 500ml (17fl oz) vegetable oil for frying

Using squid for the first time can be a little off-putting because of the look or texture. If you have a friendly fishmonger ask him to remove the guts and the clear plastic-looking quill. If you are doing it for yourself, slip a small kitchen knife under the darker outer skin and using two hands, pull the outer skin away, leaving the firm white flesh.

Method

Mix the flour with the spices and salt. Cut the bodies of the squid into 5cm (2in) squares and lightly score on one side. Remove the eye from the tentacles, then cut the tentacles into 5cm (2in) lengths. Toss the squid in the seasoned flour. Pour the oil into a frying pan so it is at least 1cm (½in) deep. Heat the oil and deep-fry the squid in batches for about 3 minutes. The flour will turn golden after about 2 minutes, then you need to fry for a further 1 minute. Lift out the squid with a slotted spoon and drain on kitchen paper. Serve with mayonnaise spiced with lime juice.

Fair Trade

'Now I belong to a co-operative, I can control my way of living. I can borrow money from the co-op when I need it at low interest rates ... safe in the knowledge that the co-op will sell my coffee for the best price and give me a dividend.'

Fried mussels with garlic and walnut sauce

Serves 4–6

900g (2lb) mussels
seasoned plain flour
1–2 eggs, lightly beaten
sunflower oil for frying
For the sauce
2 slices of stale white bread about 65g (2½oz),
  crusts removed
3 garlic cloves, crushed
1–2 tablespoons white wine vinegar
50g (2oz) Fair Trade walnuts, finely ground
salt and Fair Trade ground black pepper
6 tablespoons olive oil

Known as *midye tavasi*, this mussel dish from Turkey, created by Sophie Grigson, is sold as a street-side snack. You can make it very successfully at home though, as long as the frying oil is good and hot. The combination of sweet, hot mussels with the garlicky walnut sauce is stunning.

Method

Put some wooden skewers to soak in water for at least 30 minutes. First, make the sauce. Soak the bread in water for 10 minutes. Drain and gently squeeze out the water. Purée the bread with the garlic, vinegar, nuts and salt in a liquidizer or food processor until smooth, then gradually drizzle in the olive oil. Taste and adjust the seasoning with salt and pepper.

Next, prepare the mussels. Scrub the mussels well, scraping off the beards and small barnacles. Rinse thoroughly in several changes of water. Discard any that refuse to close when tapped sharply against a work surface, or that feel abnormally heavy (these are likely to be filled with mud and grit).

Bring 1cm (½in) of water to the boil in a large, wide pan. Add the mussels, cover tightly and shake over a high heat for a few minutes until they have opened. Discard any mussels that refuse to open. Take the mussels (the orange meat) out of their shells and reserve them.

To finish, thread the mussels on to the soaked wooden skewers. Allow about 6 mussels per skewer and don't pack them too tightly. Coat each kebab first in seasoned flour, then in beaten egg, and finally in flour again, making sure that the mussels are thoroughly coated each time. Heat the oil and fry the kebabs, turning occasionally, for about 5 minutes until golden-brown. Drain on kitchen paper and serve immediately with the sauce.

Curried haddock cakes

Serves 4

225g (8oz) smoked haddock

a knob of butter

250g (9oz) mashed potatoes

1 egg

1 teaspoon Dijon mustard

1 teaspoon mild curry paste

$\frac{1}{2}$ teaspoon Fair Trade chilli powder

$\frac{1}{2}$ teaspoon Fair Trade ground turmeric

2 turns of Fair Trade ground black pepper

a small handful of mixed fresh parsley and coriander

For the coating

75g (3oz) plain flour

2 eggs, beaten

75g (3oz) breadcrumbs

vegetable oil for frying

Method

Preheat the oven to 200°C/400°F/Gas 6. Top the haddock with the butter and cook under a hot grill for about 8 minutes until the fish can be flaked with a fork. Discard any skin or bones and mash the flesh and melted butter with the potatoes. Whisk together the egg, mustard, spices and herbs. Using a fork, blend the egg mixture into the potatoes. Shape into 8 small cakes. Coat them in flour, then in beaten egg, then finally dip them in the breadcrumbs. Heat the oil and shallow-fry the cakes for 3–4 minutes on each side until golden brown. To ensure they are cooked right through, finish off in the hot oven for 15 minutes.

Mackerel baked in tea

Serves 6

6 whole mackerel, heads removed, gutted and cleaned

6 bay leaves

1 tablespoon Fair Trade demerara sugar

12 Fair Trade black peppercorns

150ml (5fl oz) cider vinegar

150ml (5fl oz) cold Fair Trade tea

roughly chopped fresh parsley to garnish

This recipe is taken from one of several cookery books that Sara Paston-Williams has written for the National Trust. She provides excellent background information to her recipes and places many an old English dish in its context. Salting, sousing and baking mackerel in tea were Cornish ways of preserving fish in order to cope either with a sudden glut of fish, or to preserve the mackerel and broaden the diet during the winter when the fishing season stopped. This dish can be eaten hours after it comes out of the oven but is always best eaten the next day. It will become a little tired after day four.

Method

Preheat the oven to 180°C/350°F/Gas 4. Place a bay leaf inside each fish, then arrange them in an ovenproof dish. Sprinkle with the sugar and peppercorns. Mix together the vinegar and tea and pour over the fish. Cover with a lid or foil and bake in the oven for 40 minutes. Carefully lift out the fish, discard the bay leaves and arrange the fish on a serving dish. Strain over the cooking liquor and leave to cool before chilling. Sprinkle the parsley over the top and serve with warm crusty bread or a cold potato salad.

Fair Trade

'We'd like our forest to remain as it is, because it's where our source of income comes from.'

Mackerel with mustard-cauliflower salad

Serves 4

4 medium-sized mackerel fillets
salt and Fair Trade ground black pepper
120ml (4fl oz) soy sauce
2 tablespoons sesame oil

For the cauliflower salad

450g (1lb) cauliflower, cut into bite-size florets
2 red onions, sliced
1 bunch of watercress, stalks removed
2 tablespoons capers

For the dressing

1 egg yolk
3 tablespoons Dijon mustard
1 teaspoon English mustard powder blended with ½ teaspoon
   cold water
300ml (10fl oz) olive oil
juice of 1 lemon
3 teaspoons Fair Trade ground turmeric
1 teaspoon Fair Trade chilli powder

This is a Japanese-style fish salad dish. The marinade will make the mackerel skin blacken and crisp beautifully, so serve the fish skin-side up.

Method

Season the mackerel fillets with salt and pepper and place in a bowl. Mix the soy sauce and sesame oil, pour over the fish and leave to marinate.

Blanch the cauliflower in boiling salted water for 3 minutes, then drain well and leave to cool. Mix together all the salad ingredients in a bowl. Make the dressing in a food processor or use a bowl and whisk. Whisk or process the egg yolk and mustards, then slowly whisk in the oil, as you would to make a mayonnaise. Whisk in the lemon juice and spices. The dressing should be thick but it should fall off a spoon. If you need to thin it out, whisk in 1 tablespoon of cold water.

To cook the mackerel, season the fillets with salt and pepper on both sides. If you use cracked crystal salt, you will get a wonderful, crisp skin. Arrange the fillets skin-side up under a hot grill and grill for about 5 minutes. The skin will crisp and bubble. To finish the dish, toss the salad with the dressing and serve with the mackerel straight from the grill.

Spicy salmon tartare on banana chips

Makes 20

350g (12oz) fresh salmon, cut in 5mm (1/4in) dice
2 tablespoons Dijon mustard
1 tablespoon Fair Trade finely diced sun-dried mango
2 tablespoons Fair Trade chilli sauce
2 tablespoons small capers, drained
3 tablespoons spring onions, finely chopped
2 tablespoons extra virgin olive oil
salt and Fair Trade ground black pepper
250g (9oz) Fair Trade banana chips
1 tablespoon finely chopped fresh coriander leaf

Fair Trade

Canapés can often be dull and repetitive – that is something this recipe could never be accused of. It has been specially created by the chef Antony Worrall Thompson for this book. You will find that you have an excess of banana chips because for this dish you need the bigger chips from the packet. Serve the remainder in a bowl with Fair Trade mixed fruit chutney.

'The Cochabamba area of Bolivia is very poor. One thing it has in abundance, though, is top-quality bananas. A Fair Trade organization has shown local women how to dry them in solar driers ... and then export them.'

Method

Combine the first 7 ingredients and season to taste. Place a small mound of salmon on a large banana chip and sprinkle with coriander.

Noodles with spiced chicken soup

Serves 4

For the chicken

- 1 x 1.75g (4lb) chicken
- 2 teaspoons salt
- 2 onions, thinly sliced
- 3 garlic cloves, crushed
- 2.5cm (1in) piece of fresh root ginger, peeled and thinly sliced
- 1 stalk lemon grass, outer hard skin removed and thinly sliced
- 3 tablespoons Thai fish sauce (*nam pla*)
- 2 tablespoons Fair Trade palm sugar

For the soup

- 2 tablespoons sesame oil
- 2 large onions, minced
- 6 garlic cloves, crushed
- 1 teaspoon grated fresh root ginger
- 1 teaspoon Fair Trade chilli powder
- 2 tablespoons soy sauce
- 250g (9oz) fine egg noodles

To garnish

- 4 spring onions, shredded
- 175g (6oz) fine green beans, blanched and finely diced
- grated zest and juice of 2 limes
- 75g (3oz) peanuts, deep-fried
- 3 garlic cloves, very thinly sliced and deep-fried
- a small handful of fresh basil leaves, shredded

This is a wonderful Asian dish called *mowndi*. In South-east Asia, noodle soup dishes such as this can be bought, served in large clay pots, from street hawkers. The secret to the complexity of flavours is the original stock plus the last-minute addition of crisp garlic, spring onions, chopped herbs and lime juice. The garnishing peanuts and garlic are deep-fried. To save setting up a deep-fat fryer every time, it is a useful tip to have a pot with 500ml

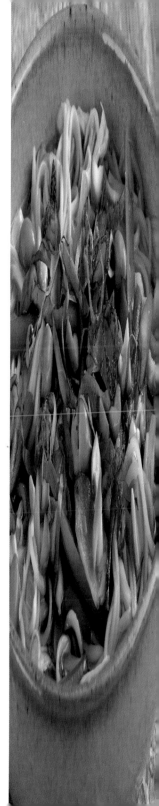

(17fl oz) of vegetable oil on the back of the stove. After each session strain out any bits.

Method

Place the whole chicken in a large pan and cover with salted water. Add the onions, garlic, ginger, lemon grass, fish sauce and sugar. Bring to the boil and skim off the scum. Cover and reduce the heat to a gentle simmer for 1 hour. Strain, reserving the liquor. Boil to reduce the liquor down to 1.75 litres (3 pints). Discard the skin and bones from the chicken and shred the meat. While the chicken is cooking, prepare the garnishes.

Heat the sesame oil in a wok and stir-fry the onions, garlic and ginger. Be vigorous and quick, stirring with a wooden spoon and allowing the ingredients just to begin to colour. Add the chilli powder and shredded chicken. Keep up a vigorous stir until the chicken is well mixed and the vegetables are coated in the chilli powder. Pour in the chicken broth and soy sauce. When the broth comes to the boil, add the noodles and cook for 2 minutes without allowing the soup to boil. Add the garnishes to the soup and serve straight away in bowls.

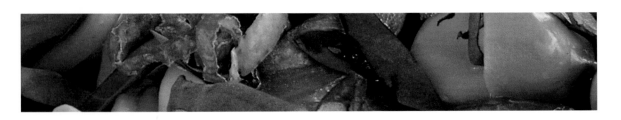

Chilled Moorish almond soup

Serves 4

- **225g (8oz) stale white bread, crusts removed**
- **3 garlic cloves**
- **3 tablespoons olive oil**
- **2 tablespoons sherry vinegar**
- **100g (4oz) Fair Trade almonds, blanched and flaked**
- **600ml (1 pint) cold water**
- **salt and Fair Trade ground black pepper**
- **grapes to garnish**

A thousand years ago, southern Spain was a part of the Moorish Empire. It was a meeting of Christian and Arabic cultures. This chilled, white almond soup, *ajo blanco*, reflects this time and its resulting influences on southern European cookery. It was created as a relief from the summer heat in the region, and makes a wonderful dish for hot summer days.

Method

Soak the bread in a bowl of water, then squeeze out the excess and tear the bread into pieces. Process in a food processor with the garlic until well blended. With the motor running, slowly pour in the oil, as you would when making mayonnaise. Add the vinegar and almonds. Slowly pour in the water until you have a creamy consistency. Season to taste with salt and pepper. Chill for at least 1 hour before serving garnished with grapes.

Cheese popadoms

Serves 4-6

75g (3oz) plain white flour
a large pinch of Fair Trade chilli powder
a pinch of Fair Trade ground black pepper
salt
1 tablespoon grated Parmesan
50g (2oz) Cheddar, grated
cold water

These biscuits or popadoms are crisp and light and make useful little garnishes for rice dishes, stews or even for snacks.

Method

Sift the flour and seasonings together. Stir in the cheeses and enough water to make a pliable dough. Chill in a fridge for at least 20 minutes.

Preheat the oven to 190°C/375°F/Gas 5 and lightly grease a baking tray. Lightly flour a work surface and roll out the dough as thinly as is possible. Cut into 4cm (1½in) diameter circles, place on the baking tray and bake in the oven for 5–7 minutes. The popadoms will darken in colour and harden when taken out of the oven, so judging the timing is important. To get it just right, practise on one to get the precise cooking time. It can be a matter of 30 seconds between just right and burnt. Leave to cool on a wire rack.

Spiced nuts

Makes 750g (1¾lb)

2 tablespoons vegetable oil

200g (7oz) Fair Trade almonds, blanched

250g (9oz) Fair Trade cashew nuts

250g (9oz) Fair Trade peanuts

75g (3oz) Fair Trade golden caster sugar

1 teaspoon ground cumin

1 teaspoon paprika

1 teaspoon Fair Trade chilli powder

salt and Fair Trade ground black pepper

This dish is best cooked over a fairly high heat to release the flavour of the spices without overcooking them. If you are doing it for the first time or are feeling a bit nervous, cook it over a medium heat and stir vigorously. The nuts will last well in an airtight container for up to two weeks but are best served the same day.

Method

Heat the oil in a heavy-based frying pan. Add the cashew nuts, almonds and peanuts. Stir the nuts around the pan using a wooden spoon for about 2 minutes until they are coated in the oil and beginning to colour. Still stirring, sprinkle in the sugar, then 30 seconds later add the spices, salt and pepper. Stir round to coat the nuts for a further 1 minute, then pour on to a plate and allow to cool.

Toffee brazils

Serves 12

225g (8oz) Fair Trade palm sugar
¹/₂ teaspoon Fair Trade ground ginger
2 tablespoons Fair Trade desiccated coconut
75g (3oz) unsalted butter, cubed
225g (8oz) Fair Trade brazil nuts

This is an adaptation of a party favourite. If you feel that the Asian influence is a step too far, then you can simply miss out the ginger and coconut. Also if you prefer straight lines and edges, then line up the brazils individually and coat them separately with the toffee, rather than cutting them out of a brick.

Fair Trade

'Each brazil nut collector is given ten trees to look after. This helps the environment, because new trees are being planted and cared for.'

Method

Melt the palm sugar in a small pan. Don't be tempted to stir or the sugar will form lumps, just shake the pan gently once or twice as the sugar melts. When all the sugar has melted you should have a dark chocolate-colour syrup. Take the pan off the heat and vigorously stir in the ginger, coconut and then the butter until the butter has melted and the toffee is smooth. Spread the brazils on a 30cm (12in) square sheet of greaseproof paper and pour over the caramel, which should have begun to cool and harden. Cut into squares or individual nuts, whichever you prefer.

Main Courses

Cashew chilli chicken

Serves 4

450g (1lb) boneless skinless chicken breasts, cut into 1cm
   (¹⁄₂in) cubes
1 egg white
1 teaspoon salt
2 teaspoons cornflour
300ml (10fl oz) groundnut or peanut oil or water
2 teaspoons groundnut or peanut oil
50g (2oz) Fair Trade cashew nuts
1 tablespoon Shaoxing rice wine or dry sherry
1 tablespoon light soy sauce
1 tablespoon Fair Trade Swazi Kitchen chilli sauce
1 tablespoon spring onions, finely chopped, to garnish

This is a recipe contributed by Ken Hom who can reproduce authentic
Asian flavours simply and with readily available ingredients.

Method

Place the cubed chicken in a small bowl and combine with the egg white,
salt and cornflour. Place in the fridge for about 20 minutes.

Heat a wok until very hot and add the oil (see below, if using water).
When the oil is very hot, remove the wok from the heat and immediately
add the chicken pieces. Stir vigorously to stop them from sticking. When the
chicken pieces turn white, after about 2 minutes, quickly drain the chicken
and excess oil over a colander set in a bowl. Discard the oil.

If you use water, bring the water to the boil in a pan. Remove the pan
from the heat and immediately add the chicken, stirring vigorously until it
turns white. Quickly drain off and discard all the water.

Heat a clean wok until it is hot, then add the 2 teaspoons of oil. Add the
cashew nuts and stir-fry for 2 minutes, then stir in the rice wine or dry
sherry, the soy and chilli sauces. Return the chicken to the pan and stir-fry
until hot and coated in the sauce. Garnish with the spring onions.

Roast chicken with rice stuffing

Serves 4

For the stuffing

> 2 tablespoons vegetable oil
>
> 1 onion, diced
>
> 2 garlic cloves, crushed
>
> 2 tablespoons Fair Trade pecans, roasted and coarsely chopped
>
> 1 tablespoon Fair Trade coarsely chopped, blanched almonds
>
> 2 tablespoons Fair Trade organic sultanas
>
> 2 tablespoons sweet sherry
>
> 50g (2oz) Fair Trade white basmati rice, cooked
>
> a handful of chopped fresh herbs (parsley, tarragon and mint)
>
> salt and Fair Trade ground black pepper

For the chicken

> 1 x 1.75kg (4lb) chicken
>
> 100g (4oz) butter, softened
>
> juice of 1 lemon
>
> 1 tablespoon vegetable oil

The stuffing will soak up a lot of the chicken juices. Serve it by the side of the meat with a plain gravy made from any juices left in the roasting tin.

Method

To make the stuffing, heat the oil and fry the onion and garlic until soft. Add the nuts and sultanas and stir for 2–3 minutes. Pour in the sherry, rice and herbs. Season with salt and pepper. Remove from the heat and cool.

Preheat the oven to 190°C/375°F/Gas 5. Fill the main cavity of the chicken with stuffing. Smear the chicken with the butter, season with salt and pepper and pour on the lemon juice. Heat the vegetable oil in a roasting tin and when it begins to smoke, place the chicken breast-side down into the tray and cook for 2 minutes. Turn the chicken over on to the other breast and cook for another 2 minutes. Turn the chicken over and you should have golden skin on the breasts. Now place the chicken in the oven for 40 minutes until cooked through, basting occasionally. Take the chicken out, cover it with foil and allow it to rest for 10 minutes before carving.

Swaziland turkey goujons

Serves 4

- 2 x 225g (8oz) turkey fillets, cut into 1 cm (1/2 in) strips
- 3 tablespoons plain flour
- 1 tablespoon Fair Trade ground ginger
- salt and Fair Trade ground black pepper
- 3 tablespoons sunflower oil

For the sauce

- 3 tablespoons oil
- 2 onions, sliced
- 2 garlic cloves, sliced
- 2 teaspoons Fair Trade sliced dried mango,
  soaked in 120ml (4fl oz) water
- 2 tablespoons Fair Trade Swazi Kitchen chilli sauce
- 2 tablespoons marmalade
- 4 tablespoons rice wine
- 1 teaspoon Fair Trade ground ginger
- 6 spring onions, sliced into 2.5cm (1in) strips

This recipe was created by Welsh TV chef Dudley Newbery.

Method

Place the meat, flour, ginger, salt and pepper in a plastic bag, hold the top firmly and shake until the meat is coated with the flour mixture. Remove the meat from the bag and shake off any excess flour. Heat the oil in a frying pan or wok and fry the meat for about 5 minutes until cooked and golden brown, then remove from the pan and keep warm.

To make the sauce, pour off any excess oil from the pan and add the fresh oil. Fry the onions and garlic on a high heat for 2–3 minutes. Lift the mango from the juice, add to the pan and cook for 1 minute. Add the mango juice, chilli sauce, marmalade, wine and ginger and cook for 4 minutes, stirring. Add the spring onions and cook for 1 minute. Serve with the turkey, accompanied by wild rice.

Yucatan-style chicken

Serves 4

12 Fair Trade black peppercorns

$1/2$ teaspoon Fair Trade dried oregano

$1/4$ teaspoon cumin seeds

2 teaspoons annatto seeds

1 teaspoon salt

Fair Trade ground black pepper

4 garlic cloves

300ml (10fl oz) Seville orange juice or $2/3$ sweet orange
juice to $1/3$ lime juice

1 x 1.75kg (4lb) chicken, quartered

banana leaves or tin foil

This is recipe from Elisabeth Lambert Ortiz's book, *Latin American Cookery*, which demonstrates the full range of Latin foods from slow-braising stews to peppery salsas. It is an ancient dish. Traditionally the chicken would be wrapped in banana leaves and baked in an earth oven known as a *pib*, hence the original name *pollo pibil*. This can be re-created in a modern kitchen using kitchen foil and a cooker. In the summer, this is perfect dish to try in the dying embers of the barbecue.

Method

Using a pestle and mortar, a blender or food processor, grind together the peppercorns, oregano, cumin seeds, annatto seeds, salt, pepper and garlic. Transfer the mixture to a large bowl and mix thoroughly with the orange juice. Add the chicken pieces and mix well to cover them with the marinade. Cover and chill for 24 hours, turning 2–3 times.

Preheat the oven to 160°C/325°F/Gas 3. Wrap each piece of chicken in a banana leaf or foil about 30cm (12in) square. Divide the marinade equally among the pieces. Arrange the packages in a casserole, cover and bake in the oven for about 2 hours or until the chicken is tender. Serve with tortillas.

Chicken with green curry, mango, lime and coconut

Serves 4

1 large teaspoon unsalted butter

1/2 teaspoon curry powder

a large pinch of Fair Trade ground turmeric

1 teaspoon Fair Trade honey

juice of 1 lime

200ml (7fl oz) tinned coconut milk

100ml (3 1/2fl oz) white chicken stock or water

1 lime leaf, fresh or dried (optional)

2 sprigs of fresh thyme

cayenne pepper or Fair Trade chilli powder

4 chicken breasts, each cut into 5 pieces, wing
  bones removed

50ml (2fl oz) double cream

1/2 green mango, peeled and diced

a handful of chopped Fair Trade cashew nuts to serve

salt and Fair Trade ground black pepper

Contributed by the renowned chef, Raymond Blanc, this recipe perfectly balances the soothing flavours of mango and coconut with the heat of the curry.

Method

Melt the butter in a small flameproof casserole, then add the curry powder and turmeric and sweat over a gentle heat for 1 minute. Add the honey and lime juice and boil for a few seconds, then add the coconut milk, chicken stock or water, lime leaf, if using, thyme, salt and cayenne pepper or chilli powder. Simmer for 2 minutes. Add the chicken pieces and cook at just under simmering point for 10 minutes until cooked. Mix in the cream, mango and cashew nuts. Season with salt and pepper.

Marinated chicken with honey and ginger served with sultana salsa

Serves 4

4 x 175g (6oz) chicken breasts with skin on

For the marinade

2 tablespoons Fair Trade clear organic honey

2.5cm (1in) cube fresh root ginger, peeled and grated

1 level teaspoon Fair Trade ground ginger

2 garlic cloves, crushed

zest and juice of 1/2 lime

salt and Fair Trade ground black pepper

For the salsa

50g (2oz) Fair Trade sultanas, soaked overnight in the zest
  and juice of 1 lime

1/2 red pepper, deseeded and chopped

1/2 medium red onion, finely chopped

1 green chilli, deseeded and finely chopped

1 medium or 1/2 large mango

1 x 15g (1/2oz) packet of coriander, leaves stripped off stems

This is a stunning recipe from Delia Smith – easy to prepare, no problem to cook and tasting absolutely divine. All you have to remember is to start the recipe the night before you want to cook it.

Method

Begin by making two cuts in each chicken breast about 5mm (1/4in) deep, then place the chicken neatly into an ovenproof dish with a base measurement of 20×15cm (8×6in) and a depth of 4.5cm (1¾in). Combine all the marinade ingredients and pour over the chicken breasts. Turn them around in the marinade to get them well coated. Cover with clingfilm and leave in the fridge overnight. In a small bowl, place the sultanas for the salsa in the zest and juice of a lime and cover with clingfilm.

When you are ready to cook the chicken, preheat the oven to 220°C/425°F/Gas 7. Remove the clingfilm from the chicken and baste with the marinade, give it a good seasoning and bake it on a high shelf of the oven for 20 minutes.

Meanwhile, remove the skin from the mango using a sharp knife or a potato peeler. Slice the flesh away from the stone and chop into 5mm (¼in) dice. Combine it with the sultanas and add the remaining salsa ingredients. Garnish with the coriander leaves. Serve the cooked chicken with the salsa as an accompaniment and perhaps some nutty brown rice.

Chicken with squash, pineapple and chilli sauce

Serves 6

2 tablespoons oil
1 large onion, chopped
4 garlic cloves, chopped
2.5cm (1in) piece of fresh root ginger, peeled and finely
   chopped
2 teaspoons cumin seeds, bruised
450–550g (1lb –1^1/$_4$lb) boneless, skinless chicken, cut into
   2.5cm (1in) pieces
675g (1^1/$_2$lb) piece orange-fleshed squash, peeled, deseeded
   and cut into cubes about the same size as the chicken
1 jar Fair Trade Swazi Kitchen chilli sauce
450g (1lb) tomatoes, skinned, deseeded and roughly chopped
salt and Fair Trade ground black pepper
^{1}/$_2$–1 pineapple, depending on size, peeled, cored and
   cut into 1cm (^{1}/$_2$in) pieces

To garnish
a handful of roughly chopped fresh coriander leaves
2 avocados, sliced
2 limes, cut into wedges

This recipe, christened chicken *eswatini*, was created for the book by Sophie
Grigson. It has a wonderfully light, sweet and spicy flavour, the fruit
balancing the chilli sauce. It is also very colourful, especially when served on
a bed of boiled rice tinged golden with a little turmeric.

Method

Heat a wok over a high heat until it smokes, then add the oil. Fry the onion
in the oil until tender and beginning to colour. Add the garlic, ginger and

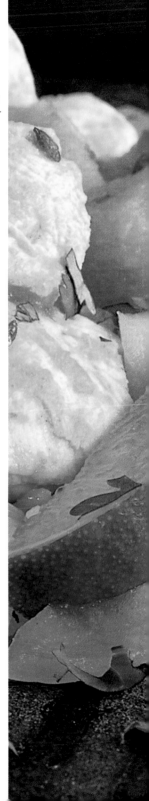

cumin seeds and fry for about 30 seconds, then tip in the chicken. Stir-fry until it turns opaque, keeping it moving to prevent it sticking. Now in goes the squash, the jar of chilli sauce, the tomatoes and just enough water to cover all the ingredients. Season with salt and pepper, bring up to the boil, then simmer gently for about 15–20 minutes until the squash is tender and the chicken is cooked. By now the sauce should have reduced to a nice thickness. If not, boil it down a little more. Stir in the pineapple, then taste and adjust the seasoning.

To serve, make a mound of golden rice on each plate, top with the chicken and scatter with coriander, then tuck a few slices of avocado in on the side. Finally, add a wedge or two of lime, then tuck in.

Duck with walnuts and orange juice

Serves 4

1 x 1.5kg (3lb) duck
salt and Fair Trade ground black pepper
1 tablespoon olive oil
300ml (10fl oz) chicken stock
150ml (5fl oz) dry sherry
225g (8oz) Fair Trade walnuts
25g (1oz) butter
600ml (1 pint) orange juice
2 teaspoons Fair Trade ground cinnamon
1/2 teaspoon Fair Trade ground ginger
1/2 teaspoon Fair Trade grated nutmeg

Using ground nuts to thicken and flavour sauces is very popular in Moorish cookery, and by using orange juice and sherry this sauce cuts through the fattiness of the duck. *Fezanjan*, as this is known, does takes time to prepare and cook but makes a perfect Sunday lunch. If you leave the duck to rest for 15 minutes once it is cooked, so much the better. The secret in cooking a duck is in the resting of the bird after the cooking so that all the juices are reabsorbed by the meat. Otherwise it is likely to be tough, tasteless and lack that wonderful pink flesh.

Method

Preheat the oven to 190°C/375°F/Gas 5. Rub the duck all over with salt and season with pepper. Heat the oil in a large ovenproof tin and brown the duck on all sides. Pour in the stock and sherry and when they come up to the boil, cover the duck with foil and cook in the middle rack of the oven for about 40 minutes until cooked through. When the duck is cooked, strain off the juices and keep the duck in a warm place while you finish the sauce.

Start the sauce while the duck is cooking. Grind the walnuts and fry them for about 1½ minutes in the butter until they darken, keeping a careful eye on the pan so that they do not burn. Pour in the orange juice and spoon in the spices. Pour the roasting juices into the sauce, bring to the boil and boil to reduce the sauce down until it is of a thick pouring consistency. Carve out the breasts and the legs and serve with boiled Fair Trade basmati rice with the sauce poured all over the meat.

Lamb biryani

Serves 6

1.5kg (3lb) lean lamb, trimmed and cut into 1cm (½in) dice
500ml (17fl oz) tinned coconut milk
550g (1½lb) Fair Trade white basmati rice

For the spice paste
½ teaspoon Fair Trade ground cinnamon
½ teaspoon Fair Trade chilli powder
1 teaspoon Fair Trade ground turmeric
½ teaspoon cloves, crushed
½ teaspoon cardamom seeds, crushed
1 teaspoon ground cumin
3 shallots
4 garlic cloves
2 teaspoons minced fresh root ginger
8 Fair Trade whole almonds, blanched

Biryani is a dish that comes in many forms – made with vegetables, meat or chicken. A meat and a rice dish all in one, it need only be served with garnishes such as raisins, spiced nuts, deep-fried garlic cloves, chillies and onions.

Method

Wash the rice and leave under running water for at least 30 minutes.

Place all the spice ingredients into a food processor and whizz into a paste. Place in a pan over a high heat and fry for 1 minute, stirring. Add the meat and stir-fry for 4 minutes. If the meat begins to stick, add a couple of tablespoons of coconut milk to the pan. Now pour in all the coconut milk, and simmer gently for 35–40 minutes to thicken the sauce.

Meanwhile place the rice in a pan of fresh water, bring to the boil, simmer for 2 minutes and then drain straight away.

Preheat the oven to 160°C/325°F/Gas 3. Pour the meat into the bottom of a large casserole, spoon on the rice and cover tightly with foil. Place the lid on top and cook in the bottom of the oven for 1 hour.

Spiced lamb

Serves 4

5 tablespoons olive oil

4 lamb loin chops

4 shallots, sliced

2 garlic cloves, crushed

juice and thinly sliced zest of 1 orange

2 sprigs of fresh thyme

2 bay leaves

1 teaspoon Fair Trade dried oregano

1 teaspoon salt

1 teaspoon Fair Trade ground black pepper

1 teaspoon paprika

1 teaspoon ground cumin

1 teaspoon Fair Trade demerara sugar

2 teaspoons tomato purée

2 glasses red wine

4 tomatoes, skinned and diced

2 tablespoons coarsely chopped fresh flatleaf parsley

Method

Heat 2 tablespoons of olive oil in an ovenproof frying pan. Add the chops and sear them for 4 minutes on each side, by which time they should be beginning to crisp and certainly be a golden-brown colour. If not, give them a couple more minutes cooking each side. Remove the chops from the pan and discard the fat.

Preheat the oven to 200°C/400°F/Gas 6. Using the same pan, heat the remaining olive oil. Now you will have to work fairly quickly to avoid burning the spices. In the oil, fry the shallots and the garlic until they begin to brown. Then quickly throw in the orange zest, herbs, salt, pepper, spices and sugar, give a quick stir, then spoon in the tomato purée. Again, keep stirring, and cook the paste until it begins to stick. Immediately pour in the wine, orange juice and diced tomato. Bring the liquor back to the boil. Turn down the heat and return the lamb to the pan, making sure that the chops are covered in sauce. Bring back up to the bubble, loosely cover with foil and bake in the oven for a further 6–10 minutes (6 minutes for rare, 10 minutes for cooked all the way through). If it looks as though the sauce may stick, add a touch of water. Remove the lamb from the oven and leave to rest covered with foil for a few minutes while you finish off the rest of the preparation for the meal. Sprinkle with parsley and serve with Fair Trade white basmati rice.

Fair Trade

'Before you finish eating your breakfast this morning, you've depended on half the world. This is the way our universe is structured ... We aren't going to have peace on earth until we recognise this basic fact.' Martin Luther King

Tagine of lamb or mutton with fruit and almonds

Serves 5-6

1-1.25 kg (2¼-2¾lb) boned shoulder of lamb or mutton
50 g (2oz) unsalted butter
2 tablespoons oil
2¼ teaspoons ground saffron
1 teaspoon Fair Trade ground black pepper
salt
1 teaspoon Fair Trade ground ginger
1 teaspoon ground cumin
½ tablespoon Fair Trade ground cinnamon
2 medium onions, grated or very finely chopped
225g (8oz) prunes
175g (6oz) Fair Trade dried apricots
1 tablespoon sesame seeds
1 cinnamon stick
2 long strips lemon zest
2-3 tablespoons Fair Trade honey
75g (3oz) Fair Trade almonds, blanched and halved

Moroccan *tagines* take their name from the beautiful wide dishes with conical lids in which they are cooked. They are highly aromatic, often combining fruit with meat, and sometimes sweetened with honey. This recipe from Sophie Grigson is richly but not overwhelmingly spiced and finished with the crunch of fried almonds and sesame seeds. If you prefer, you can use 450g (1lb) of prunes alone or 350g (12oz) of apricots alone. Only bother to soak the fruit if it is bone dry.

Method

Cut the lamb or mutton into 4cm (1½in) cubes, trimming off any gristle and excess fat. Melt 40g (1½oz) of the butter and mix it with the oil, saffron, pepper, salt, ginger, cumin and cinnamon and coat the lamb in the mixture. Tip into a wide frying pan or shallow flameproof casserole and cook over a moderate heat for about 3 minutes to toast the spices. Add the onions and enough water just to cover the ingredients. Bring to the boil, partially cover, then simmer gently for 1–2 hours or until the meat is tender.

If necessary, soak the prunes and apricots in water. The prunes can be stoned if you wish, but it's not really necessary. Dry-fry the sesame seeds in small pan over a high heat until they turn a shade darker, shaking the pan and watching carefully as they can burn easily. If it has been soaked, drain the dried fruit. Add to the meat, along with the cinnamon stick, lemon zest and honey. Simmer, uncovered, for a further 30 minutes or so until the sauce has reduced enough to coat the meat and fruit without leaving them swimming (you may even have to add a little water if yours seems to have evaporated too quickly). While it simmers, sauté the almonds in the remaining butter until they are lightly browned, then set aside and keep warm. Taste the tagine and adjust the seasonings. Finally, scatter with the almonds and sesame seeds before serving.

Lamb satay

Serves 4

For the sauce

- 2 shallots
- 1 garlic clove
- 1 teaspoon *terasi* (fermented shrimp paste)
- a pinch of Fair Trade chilli powder
- salt and Fair Trade ground black pepper
- 1 tablespoon sesame oil
- 500ml (17fl oz) water
- 100g (4oz) Fair Trade peanut butter
- juice of 1 lemon
- 1 tablespoon Fair Trade palm sugar
- 1kg (2¼lb) leg or shoulder of lamb, or beef joint

For the marinade

- 2 shallots
- 1 garlic clove, crushed
- 2 tablespoons soy sauce
- a pinch of Fair Trade chilli powder
- 1 teaspoon ground coriander
- 1 teaspoon Fair Trade ground ginger
- juice of 1 lemon
- 1 tablespoon vegetable oil

Fair Trade

Peanut butter is made from peanuts imported from India, Africa and Nicaragua. As there has been a fluctuation in the supply of the peanuts, Oxfam is working with a local Senegal organization supporting small-scale farmers to develop a new source.

Method

Make the sauce in advance. Purée the shallots, garlic and *terasi*. Add the chilli powder, salt and pepper. Heat the oil in a pan and fry the shallot pulp until it starts to colour. Pour in the water and bring to the boil. Add the peanut butter, lemon juice and sugar and stir for 2–3 minutes until the sauce thickens.

Slice the meat into thin, finger-length pieces. Mix all the marinade ingredients with the meat and marinate overnight or for at least 3 hours. Once marinated, thread the meat along skewers in a wave pattern. Cook the meat under a hot grill for 6 minutes on each side. Serve hot with the sauce and with boiled rice.

Ghanaian pumpkin

Serves 4

- 1 aubergine, diced
- 50ml (2fl oz) vegetable oil
- 1 onion, roughly chopped
- 450g (1lb) minced beef
- ½ teaspoon Fair Trade chilli powder
- ½ teaspoon ground coriander
- 1 green pepper, deseeded and roughly chopped
- 900g (2lb) pumpkin, diced
- 2 ripe tomatoes
- salt and Fair Trade ground black pepper

Ponkie is the Ghanaian for pumpkin and the traditional name of this recipe. It was contributed by Ola Olaore, from her book *Traditional African Cookery*. Pumpkin is one of the staple foods of Ghana and so is used in many different and interesting ways.

Method

Put the aubergine to soak in salted water. Heat the oil in a pan and lightly fry the onion until soft. Add the minced beef and spices and cook for 10 minutes until the mince is a healthy brown colour. Stir in the pepper, pumpkin and tomatoes. Drain the aubergine and stir it in. Bring to a simmer, lower the heat and cook gently for 20 minutes, stirring occasionally. Season with salt and pepper. Serve hot with Fair Trade white basmati rice or with boiled yam.

Fair Trade

'... sometimes economic pressures can make you short-sighted and tempt you to take too much from the land now and let the next generation pay the price.'

Beef and rice omelette

Serves 4–6

- 3 tablespoons olive or peanut oil
- 5 shallots, finely chopped
- 3 garlic cloves, finely chopped
- 1 teaspoon Fair Trade chilli powder
- 1/2 teaspoon salt
- 1/2 teaspoon Fair Trade ground black pepper
- 100g (4oz) cooked beef, thinly sliced and cut into small pieces
- 65g (2 1/2 oz) long-grain rice, cooked
- 1 tablespoon Fair Trade desiccated coconut
- 5 duck eggs or 7 hen eggs

Sri Owen was brought up amongst the rice fields. *The Rice Book* has been rightly billed as the definitive book on the magic of rice cooking. It is from this book that this recipe is taken. In principle, this omelette is the Indonesian version of a Spanish omelette in that it is thick, well browned and crusty on the outside and soft inside. Sri Owen suggests using the meat from the Rhubarb Khoresh (see page 72), but you can use any boiled or roast beef or salt beef from your local delicatessen.

Method

Heat 2 tablespoons of the oil in a frying pan and stir-fry the shallots and garlic for 3–4 minutes. Add all the other ingredients except the eggs. Stir-fry and mix for a further 2 minutes. Beat the eggs in a bowl. Transfer the mixture from the pan to the bowl with the beaten eggs and mix everything very well. Adjust the seasoning with salt and pepper. Brush the pan with remaining oil and set it on a low heat. When the pan is hot, pour the mixture into it and cook, shaking the pan from time to time, for 3–4 minutes until the top is set but not quite cooked. Using oven gloves, cover the pan with a plate and invert the omelette on to the plate. Slide it back into the pan and continue to cook for a further 2 minutes until the other side is set. Turn off the heat, cover the pan and leave the omelette to rest. Uncover while the omelette is still warm, cut into 4–6 pieces and serve straight away.

Devilled kidneys with bean hot pot

Serves 4

450g (1lb) dried green haricot beans, soaked overnight
50g (2oz) olive oil
3 onions, sliced
4 garlic cloves, crushed
1 teaspoon Fair Trade dried oregano
500ml (17fl oz) passata
600ml (1 pint) beef or chicken stock
2 teaspoons harissa or chilli paste
2 tablespoons Dijon mustard
1 teaspoon English mustard mixed to a paste
  with 1 teaspoon water
1 teaspoon Fair Trade ground ginger
350g (12oz) calves' kidneys, trimmed
50g (2oz) plain flour
2 teaspoons Fair Trade chilli powder
1 teaspoon salt
1 teaspoon Fair Trade ground black pepper
2 tablespoons olive oil
1 tablespoon red wine vinegar (optional)

This is a rich, warming and inexpensive dish. The portion size is large and the dish is filling. It is best eaten with hot baguette to mop up the juices.

Method

Drain the beans from their soaking liquid, place them in a large flameproof casserole dish and cover with fresh cold water. It is important not to add salt at this stage as it will stop the beans absorbing the water and they will end up as hard as pebbles. Bring to the boil and skim off any scum that rises to the surface. Cover and reduce the heat to a slow simmer for up to 2 hours until the beans are tender, then strain the beans out of the casserole.

Preheat the oven to 150°C/300°F/Gas 2. Heat the oil in the same dish and fry the onions and garlic until just beginning to colour. Stir in the beans, oregano and passata and cook for 1–2 minutes, stirring to coat the beans in the sauce. Add the stock and return to the boil. Remove from the heat and stir in the harissa or chilli paste, mustards and ginger.

Slice the kidneys into 5mm (¼in) discs. Mix the flour with the chilli powder, salt and pepper. Toss the kidneys in the seasoned flour. Heat the olive oil in a frying pan. Shake off any excess flour from the kidneys and, when the oil is smoking, fry the kidneys for 1 minute only on each side. Spoon out the kidneys and place on the beans. If you have the nerve, de-glaze the frying pan with the red wine vinegar (it will sizzle and splutter) and pour the juices into the pot as well. Put a lid on the casserole and place in the bottom of the oven for 1 hour. At this point the beans just begin to simmer.

Baharat

Makes 7 teaspoons

- 1 teaspoon cloves
- 1 teaspoon coriander seeds
- 3 cardamom seeds
- 1 teaspoon Fair Trade ground black pepper
- 1 teaspoon Fair Trade ground cinnamon
- 1 teaspoon Fair Trade grated nutmeg
- 1/2 teaspoon Fair Trade chilli power
- 1 teaspoon paprika

This is a typical Middle Eastern spice used to flavour barbecued meat and fish. Although it would be easier to make up a large batch, ground spices lose their edge after one month so only make what you can use in that time.

Method

Using a pestle and mortar or food processor, grind the cloves, coriander and cardamom seeds. Grind in the remaining ingredients. Store in an airtight jar.

Barbecued fish with dates

Serves 6

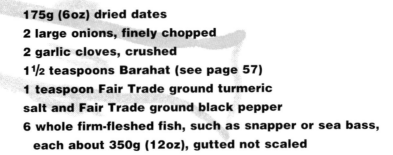

175g (6oz) dried dates
2 large onions, finely chopped
2 garlic cloves, crushed
1½ teaspoons Barahat (see page 57)
1 teaspoon Fair Trade ground turmeric
salt and Fair Trade ground black pepper
6 whole firm-fleshed fish, such as snapper or sea bass,
each about 350g (12oz), gutted not scaled

Fair Trade

'In the case of Peru, Fair Trade is helping to limit the spread of crops like coca, from which cocaine is derived. In Peru this is a traditional crop and, when the peasant farmers find themselves in difficult economic situations, they have little alternative but to grow coca. This does a lot of harm, not only in our countries but also all over the world.'

Tess Mallos contributed this recipe to an encyclopedia of a book called *The Complete Middle East Cookbook*. It is from there that this Gulf State dish comes. The traditional Gulf way to grill fish is in a special cut-away, dome-shaped clay barbecue with glowing coals in the base, but it is fine to use a normal barbecue at home. The scales keep the flesh intact and the skin is removed before eating. The dates give the fish a very pleasant flavour.

Method

Put the dates in water to soak for 30 minutes until soft. Mix together the onions, garlic and spices and a little water to make a paste. Season with salt and pepper. Wash out the cavities of the fish and fill them with the stuffing. Close the cavity with a cocktail stick that has been soaked in water.

Purée the dates in a liquidizer, using a little water if necessary. Spread the purée on the sides of the fish and leave on a rack for 10 minutes. Cook the fish over charcoal for 4–5 minutes each side, depending on the thickness of the flesh.

Kedgeree

Serves 4

For the fish stock

1.5kg (3lb) fish bones, including heads

1.75 litres (3 pints) water

a handful of button mushrooms, sliced

1 large onion, chopped

1 large leek, chopped

1 large carrot, chopped

1 celery stick, including the leafy top, sliced

For the court bouillon

300ml (10fl oz) milk

600ml (1 pint) water

1 medium onion, thinly sliced

2 bay leaves

6 Fair Trade black peppercorns

$\frac{1}{2}$ lemon, sliced

350g (12oz) smoked haddock fillet

For the rice

40g (1$\frac{1}{2}$oz) butter

a large pinch of Fair Trade ground turmeric

1 clove

1 cardamom pod

275g (10oz) Fair Trade white basmati rice

600ml (1 pint) fish stock from above

$\frac{1}{2}$ teaspoon salt

2 tablespoons chopped fresh parsley

3 hard-boiled eggs, coarsely chopped

'There's a hint of Indian spice in my kedgeree,' says Rick Stein, 'not enough to put you off your breakfast, but just enough to serve as a faint reminder of where this dish came from.'

Method

First make the fish stock by placing the fish bones in the water and bringing to the boil. Simmer for 20 minutes, then pass through a strainer lined with muslin. Return the stock to the pan and add the vegetables. Bring to the boil and simmer again for 45 minutes. Strain again and use or store for up to 4 days in a covered container in the fridge.

Next make the court bouillon. Place all the ingredients, except the fish, in a pan and bring to the boil, then simmer for 10 minutes. Add the haddock and cook for 8–12 minutes until cooked, depending on the thickness of the fillet. Remove from the pan and drain. Remove the skin and any bones and break the fish up in to finger-sized pieces. Keep it warm.

Preheat the oven to 200°C/400°F/Gas 6. Sweat the butter, turmeric, clove and cardamom together in a flameproof pan, stir in the rice and cook for 1 minute, then pour in the stock, add the salt and bring to the boil. Cover and cook in the oven for 17 minutes. Remove the rice from the oven and fold in the fish, parsley and eggs gently to avoid breaking them up. Season with salt and serve immediately.

Warm Thai mussel salad with mint

Serves 4

1.5kg (3lb) mussels
2 garlic cloves
2 tablespoons peanut oil
250ml (8fl oz) dry white wine
6 black peppercorns
4 coriander stems
1 teaspoon Fair Trade palm or cane sugar
juice of 1 lime or lemon
2 tablespoons Thai fish sauce (*nam pla*)
5 tablespoons coconut milk
1 teaspoon grated fresh root ginger
1/2–1 fresh red chilli, thinly sliced
Fair Trade ground black pepper
4 tablespoons fresh mint leaves

An easy play on Thai flavourings. Serve this Jill Dupleix recipe warm with steamed jasmine rice, or leave to cool and serve as a tangy, spicy salad.

Method

Soak the mussels in cold water for 3–4 hours, changing the water twice. Discard any mussels with broken shells, any that float or do not close when tapped sharply. Scrub the shells clean under cold running water and pull off the beards. Crush 1 garlic clove and leave the other whole.

Heat the oil in a lidded frying pan and fry the garlic until coloured. Add the wine, peppercorns and coriander stems and bring to the boil. Add the mussels, cover tightly and turn up the heat. Shake the pan vigorously for 2–3 minutes, then remove the open mussels, discarding any that do not open. Strain the cooking juices through a fine strainer or muslin cloth, and place the mussels in a serving bowl.

Combine cooking juices, sugar, lime or lemon juice, fish sauce, coconut milk, ginger, chilli and pepper in a saucepan and heat gently, stirring. Pour over the mussels, add mint and toss lightly.

Nasi goreng

Serves 4

- 5 tablespoons vegetable oil
- 2 eggs, beaten
- 2 shallots, thinly sliced
- 2 carrots, finely diced
- 250g (9oz) white cabbage, shredded
- 2 garlic cloves, chopped
- 2 small chillies, deseeded and thinly sliced
- 75g (3oz) peanuts, toasted
- 100g (4oz) frozen peas
- 2 spring onions, thinly sliced
- 225g (8oz) Fair Trade white basmati rice, boiled
- 50ml (2fl oz) soy sauce
- 3 tablespoons mirin
- 1 tablespoon Fair Trade Swazi Kitchen chilli sauce
- 4 fried eggs (optional)

The literal translation of *nasi goreng* is fried rice. It is an Indonesian dish that is a great way of using up leftover vegetables and rice, so use this recipe as a guide rather than a rule book.

Method

First make an omelette. Heat 1 tablespoon of oil in a wok, ensuring you have plenty of space for vigorous stirring. Pour in the beaten eggs and when they begin to set, turn the omelette over and cook for a further 30 seconds. Remove the omelette from the pan and shred into finger-size slices.

Pour the remaining oil into the wok. Add the carrots and cabbage and stir-fry until the cabbage is well on the way to being wilted. Stir in the garlic, chillies, nuts and peas and stir around the pan for 5 minutes. Then add the spring onions, rice, soy sauce, mirin and chilli sauce. Mix thoroughly and when the rice is hot, stir in the shredded omelette. Serve it as you would have it in Indonesia, in a bowl with a fried egg on top.

Leek and almond filo pie

Serves 6

225g (8oz) butter
3 garlic cloves, crushed
900g (2lb) trimmed leeks, thinly sliced
1 tablespoon Fair Trade dried basil
100g (4oz) Fair Trade almonds, blanched and ground
175g (6oz) goats' cheese
250g (9oz) filo pastry

For the watercress sauce

25g (1oz) butter
4 shallots, finely diced
1 teaspoon Dijon mustard
175ml (6fl oz) vegetable stock
50ml (2fl oz) double cream
4 bunches of watercress, stalks removed

This dish, from chef Don Hacker, is rich, moist and has buckets of flavour.

Method

To make the filling, melt half the butter in a pan, add the garlic, leeks and basil and cook over a low heat for 10 minutes until the leeks are soft but not stewed. Stir in the almonds and goats' cheese. Allow to cool.

Preheat the oven to 190°C/375°F/Gas 5 and grease a 23cm (9in) flan tin. Melt the remaining butter, brush it over the filo sheets and layer them in the tin. Spoon in the filling and twist up the filo to meet in the centre. Bake in the centre of the oven for 30–35 minutes.

To make the sauce, melt the butter in a pan and fry the shallots until soft. Pour in the mustard, stock and cream. Bring to the boil, then simmer for 5 minutes. Remove from the heat and add the watercress leaves. Before the watercress has a chance to lose its wonderful green colour, blitz the sauce in a food processor until completely smooth, then pass through the finest sieve you have. Serve the filo parcel in wedges with the sauce ready to pour from a jug.

Pea and hazelnut stew

Serves 4

450g (1lb) fresh shelled peas
300ml (10fl oz) vegetable stock
50g (2oz) Fair Trade desiccated coconut
2 tablespoons sesame oil
250g (9oz) Fair Trade hazelnuts, roughly chopped
2 garlic cloves, chopped
1 red pepper, deseeded and chopped into 5mm ($1/4$ in) dice
2 teaspoons minced fresh root ginger
$1/4$ teaspoon garam masala
1 teaspoon rice flour
1 tablespoon Thai fish sauce (*nam pla*)
4 spring onions, sliced
a handful of fresh mint and coriander leaves, lightly chopped
salt and Fair Trade ground black pepper

This dish is full of colour and full of life. It is perfectly finished off with plain boiled rice or egg noodles to soak up the juices.

Method

Boil the peas rapidly in the stock for 1 minute. Drain, reserving the liquor in a mixing bowl. Into this liquor, whisk the desiccated coconut for 2–3 minutes, which will help to melt the coconut. Heat the oil in a frying pan. Add the nuts and brown them, continually moving the pan. Add the garlic and pepper and fry until the garlic begins to colour. Stir in the ginger, garam masala and rice flour and just as it begins to stick, pour in the pea stock and the fish sauce. Bring to a vigorous bubble and cook for 4 minutes to cook the peas and reduce the liquor. Add the spring onions and mint and coriander and serve in bowls with either egg noodles or boiled rice.

Chicory tatin

Serves 4

450g (1lb) puff pastry

100g (4oz) butter

4 heads of chicory, halved

1 teaspoon Fair Trade ground cinnamon

1 teaspoon Fair Trade ground ginger

1 tablespoon Fair Trade honey with orange juice

juice of 1 orange

1 tablespoon dry sherry

50g (2oz) Parmesan, grated

The sweet and sour flavour created by caramelizing the chicory is very refreshing. Serve with a well-dressed mixed leaf salad.

Method

Divide the pastry into quarters. Roll out each piece to a 10×15cm (4×6in) rectangle. Place each pastry on a separate piece of baking parchment and put them into the fridge until needed.

Melt the butter in a large frying pan. Place the chicory, cut-side down, in the pan so they all touch the bottom of the pan and brown for 3 minutes. Turn them over and stir in the cinnamon and ginger. Pour in the honey, orange juice and sherry, bring to the boil, then reduce the heat to a gentle simmer and cook for a further 15 minutes. Remove the chicory from the pan and boil to reduce the liquid until it becomes a syrup. Cool, then place both the syrup and the chicory in the fridge to chill.

Preheat the oven to 220°C/425°F/Gas 7. Spoon a tablespoon of the set syrup into the centre of each pastry. On to this place 2 chicory halves and on to that sprinkle a little of the Parmesan. Bake in the hot oven for 12–15 minutes. The sides of the pastry will puff up and will hold the majority of the syrup in place.

Fair Trade

Only Fair Trade guarantees a minimum price to producers... 'We want a stable market, not just now, but for the future, to allow us to negotiate a fair price that secures a decent standard of living.'

Millet gratin

Serves 4

400g (14oz) millet, washed
salt
50g (2oz) butter
2 tablespoons olive oil
3 onions, roughly chopped
3 tomatoes, skinned and roughly chopped
50g (2oz) Fair Trade Maya Gold dark chocolate, broken up
2 garlic cloves, sliced
1 teaspoon Fair Trade dried oregano
1 teaspoon ground cumin
1 teaspoon paprika
1 teaspoon Fair Trade chilli powder
300ml (10fl oz) passata
750g (1¾lb) minced pork
olive oil
50g (2oz) green olives, stoned
175g (6oz) Cheddar, grated

This sauce recipe from Oxfam Belgique contains chocolate, which not only gives the sauce a wonderful rich colour but takes the edge off the chilli. This is a common practice in South American cooking where chillies have fire and kick.

Method

Measure water to double the volume of the millet into a pan, about 900ml (1½ pints), add a little salt and bring to the boil. Pour in the washed millet, return to the boil, then simmer for 25 minutes, by which time all the liquid will have been absorbed. Add the butter and remove from the heat.

Heat the oil and fry the onions for about 3 minutes. Add the tomatoes, chocolate, garlic, oregano, spices and passata and mix gently. Cover and cook for 15 minutes. In a separate pan, fry the mince in a little oil until browned, then add it to the sauce.

Preheat the oven to 200°C/400°F/Gas 6 and grease a large ovenproof dish. Pour in half the cooked millet. Pour in the sauce and scatter on the olives. Cover with the remaining millet. Sprinkle over the cheese and bake in the oven for 15 minutes. To finish the gratin, place it under a hot grill for a few minutes to brown the cheese.

Fruit curry

Serves 6

3 baking potatoes, diced

1 onion, chopped

375g (13oz) cooking apples or Granny Smiths, peeled, cored
  and diced

1 large banana, chopped

2–3 carrots, sliced

400g (14oz) tinned chopped tomatoes

425g (15oz) Fair Trade mango chutney

450ml (15fl oz) bio yoghurt

2 tablespoons mild curry powder

2 tablespoons tikka paste

40g (1$\frac{1}{2}$oz) Fair Trade desiccated coconut

2 garlic cloves, crushed

bay leaves to garnish

This appeared in a previous collection of recipes by vegetarian cook Rose Elliot. It is very colourful, nutritionally balanced and easy to prepare.

Method

Simply place all the ingredients in a large pan, cover and simmer over a low heat for 2–3 hours. Remove the lid for the last 30 minutes if there is too much liquid. Serve on a bed of boiled rice and peas, garnished with a few bay leaves.

Millet balls

Serves 4

275g (10oz) millet, washed
salt
1 egg
1 teaspoon Fair Trade dried basil
a pinch of Fair Trade chilli powder
225g (8oz) Cheddar, grated
oil for deep-frying

For the sauce

100g (4oz) Fair Trade cashew nuts
150ml (5fl oz) milk
4 tablespoons olive oil
2 onions, chopped
2 garlic cloves, chopped
1 teaspoon Fair Trade chilli powder
1 teaspoon paprika
120ml (4fl oz) bio yoghurt
Fair Trade ground black pepper

For the garnish

100g (4oz) black olives
3 hard-boiled eggs, quartered
1 cos lettuce, shredded

Method

Measure water to double the volume of the millet into a pan, about 750ml (1¼ pints), add a little salt and bring to the boil. Pour in the washed millet, return to the boil, then simmer for 20 minutes, by which time all the liquid will have been absorbed.

Beat the egg with the basil and chilli powder and add it to the cheese. Stir this thoroughly into the hot millet, then leave to cool. Shape the mixture into 8 balls. Deep-fry in hot oil in batches of 2 or 3 until browned, then set to one side.

To make the sauce, purée the cashew nuts and milk to a paste in a food processor. Heat half the olive oil and fry the nut purée for 2 minutes. Spoon out the nuts and give the pan a quick wipe. In the same pan, heat the remaining oil and fry the onions and garlic until soft. Add the chilli powder and paprika and fry for a few minutes. Add the nut paste and yoghurt and cook for 1 minute. Do not allow the sauce to come to the boil. The balls should be served cold, covered with the hot sauce. Garnish with the olives, eggs and lettuce dressed simply with a lemon and olive oil dressing.

Yoghurt and cashew pasta sauce

Serves 2

- **4 tablespoons olive oil**
- **1 onion, sliced**
- **1 garlic clove, chopped**
- **100g (4oz) Fair Trade cashew nuts, roasted**
- **1 teaspoon Fair Trade chilli powder**
- **1 teaspoon Fair Trade dried basil**
- **250ml (8fl oz) bio yoghurt**
- **juice of 1 lemon**
- **salt and Fair Trade ground black pepper**
- **a small handful of chopped fresh mint**

This dish makes a light lunch-time meal and is an example of low-fat cooking with a high flavour value.

Method

Heat the oil and fry the onion and garlic until soft, then add the nuts, chilli powder and basil and cook for a further 2 minutes. Pour in the yoghurt and lemon juice and season with salt and pepper. Keep stirring until the yoghurt is warmed through but do not allow it to boil. Remove from the heat, stir in the mint and it is ready to serve with pasta such as tagliatelle.

Rhubarb khoresh

Serves 4

- 2–3 tablespoons oil or butter
- 3 shallots, chopped
- 2 garlic cloves, chopped
- 450g (1lb) brisket or stewing meat, fat removed and diced
- ½ teaspoon Fair Trade chilli powder
- ½ teaspoon Fair Trade ground cinnamon
- 1 teaspoon salt and Fair Trade ground black pepper
- 900ml (1½ pints) hot water, more to hand if needed
- 225g (8oz) rhubarb

It may seem a little unusual to use rhubarb in a main course dish but it provides a perfect sweet-sour balance that is so common in Asian dishes. This recipe comes from Sri Owen's *The Rice Book* and she suggests serving it with plain boiled rice. Also, which is an excellent idea, she suggests utilizing the strained meat from the Beef and Rice Omelette (see page 55).

Method

Heat the oil or butter in a pan and fry the shallots and garlic until soft. Add the beef and stir-fry for 2 minutes. Add the chilli powder, cinnamon, salt and pepper and continue stir-frying for 1 minute. Add the hot water, bring to the boil and skim off any scum. Let the mixture boil for about 10 minutes, then lower the heat, cover the pan and simmer for 1½ hours. Uncover several times to check the water level and add water at the halfway mark if required.

While the meat is cooking, wash and cut up the rhubarb into small pieces and keep to one side. About 10 minutes before the cooking is finished, pour the khoresh into a bowl and then back into the pan through a sieve to remove the meat. Discard the meat. Add the rhubarb and cook for a further 10 minutes. Adjust the seasoning and serve with boiled rice.

Fair Trade

'The income we get from coffee clothes us, pays for school fees, and buys seed and implements.'

Vegetables and Salads

Spiced mixed vegetables with coconut

Serves 4

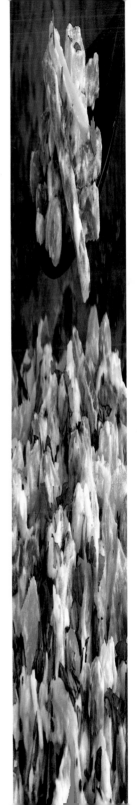

- 350g (12oz) green beans, trimmed and halved
- 2 carrots, diced
- 175g (6oz) fresh or frozen peas
- 250ml (8fl oz) water
- 1 medium-sized potato, boiled, peeled and diced
- 75g (3oz) Fair Trade sun-dried mango, thinly sliced
- 1–2 fresh hot chillies, finely chopped
- 75g (3oz) Fair Trade desiccated coconut
- 2 tablespoons vegetable oil
- a generous pinch of ground asafoetida
- 1 teaspoon black mustard seeds
- 1 teaspoon cumin seeds
- 2 tablespoons urad dal
- 350ml (12fl oz) plain yoghurt
- 2 teaspoons salt
- 2 tablespoons finely chopped fresh coriander

This is a mixed vegetable dish, called *aviyal*, from the south-west of India. It comes from Madhur Jaffrey's book, *Eastern Vegetarian Cooking*. Don't be put off by the long list of ingredients, it is only a guide to show the amount and balance of vegetables to be used. This dish is supposed to use up all the excess vegetables you have in store and is a good one to play around with. The results are well worth the effort.

Method

Combine the beans, carrots and peas in a small pan, add the water and bring to the boil. Cover, lower the heat and cook for 4–5 minutes or until the vegetables are tender but still crunchy and almost all the water has been absorbed. Combine the cooked vegetables with the potato and mango in a wide heavy pan. Sprinkle with the chillies and coconut.

Heat the oil in a small, heavy frying pan. When hot, put in the asafoetida and a few seconds later, the mustard seeds and cumin seeds. As soon as the mustard seeds begin to pop, put in the urad dal. Stir and fry until the dal turns a light reddish-brown. Pour over the cooked vegetables.

Empty the yoghurt into a bowl and mix with a fork. Add the salt and mix again. Pour the yoghurt over the vegetables and place the pan over a low heat. Heat the vegetables, stirring gently until warmed thoroughly. Don't allow the mixture to boil. Sprinkle with the fresh coriander and serve warm.

Dodo with peanuts

Serves 4

1 teaspoon Fair Trade palm sugar
1 teaspoon Fair Trade ground ginger
1 teaspoon Fair Trade ground cinnamon
a pinch of salt and Fair Trade ground black pepper
3 plantains, peeled and diagonally sliced to finger thickness
4 tablespoons sunflower oil
75g (3oz) peanuts
2 tablespoons Fair Trade desiccated coconut

Having a sweet-tasting side dish is a common feature in African cooking. It is used to balance the taste of a bitter or sour main dish, or even to counter the heat of a chilli dish.

Method

Mix together the sugar and spices, salt and pepper and roll the plantains in the mixture to season. Heat the oil in a large frying pan. Throw in the peanuts and stir with a wooden spoon for a few minutes until they begin to colour. Using a slotted spoon, scoop the peanuts out and set aside. In the same pan, fry the plantains for 2–3 minutes on each side. Gently remove from the pan and place on a serving plate with the peanuts. Sprinkle all over with the coconut before serving.

Honey-roasted vegetables

Serves 4

2 carrots

2 parsnips

1 turnip

2 leeks

2 celery sticks

450g (1lb) new potatoes

4 garlic cloves

4 tablespoons olive oil

2 tablespoons Fair Trade clear organic honey

1 teaspoon Fair Trade dried oregano

2 bay leaves

2 teaspoons lemon juice

salt and Fair Trade ground black pepper

As well as going well with the Sunday roast, these vegetables can be served as a starter with pasta dressed with flavoured oil. To achieve crispy vegetables sear them before roasting, and then disturb them as little as possible.

Method

Preheat the oven to 200°C/400°F/Gas 6. With the exception of the potatoes, cut the vegetables across at an angle into 2cm (¾ in) ovals. Cut the potatoes into 1cm (½ in) ovals. Blanch in boiling salted water for 1 minute. Drain and place the vegetables and the garlic in a hot flameproof roasting tray with the olive oil.

Heat the vegetables over a high heat, turning them over to ensure they begin to colour evenly. This should only take 5 minutes. Bake in the oven for 30 minutes, turning only once or at the most twice. Spoon in the honey, oregano and bay leaves and turn the vegetables until they have an even coating of oil and honey. Put back in the oven for a further 30 minutes. The result you want is a golden, crispy skin. When the vegetables come out of the oven, sprinkle with the lemon juice and season to taste with salt and pepper.

Fair Trade

Oregano and basil are grown and dried in Ethiopia and packed in England. The Ethiopian Gemini Trust was established to help very poor families with twins or triplets. It provides care, education and job opportunities. Processing of locally grown herbs and spices was begun with the support of the Oxfam office in Addis Ababa.

Kachumber salad

Serves 4

3 tomatoes, halved and thinly sliced
1 medium-sized onion, halved and thinly sliced
2 tablespoons chopped fresh coriander
1/4 teaspoon ground cumin
1/8 teaspoon Fair Trade chilli powder
2 tablespoons white wine vinegar
1/2 teaspoon salt

This is an Indian recipe that freshens the mouth after the heat of a curry.

Method

Mix together all the ingredients in a bowl and serve.

Gujarati-style yoghurt with potatoes

Serves 4–6

olive oil
1/2 teaspoon cumin seeds
450g (1lb) new potatoes, boiled, peeled and diced
250ml (8fl oz) plain yoghurt
1 tablespoon chopped fresh coriander
1/2 teaspoon salt and Fair Trade ground black pepper
a pinch of Fair Trade chilli powder

Indian cookery is very regionally based with each district having its own individual style. Gujarati cuisine is very strong on vegetarian dishes and as can be seen from this recipe, *batata nu raita*, taken from Lindsey Bareham's *In Praise of the Potato*, they are often well-spiced and tempered with yoghurt.

Method

Heat a little oil in a pan and fry the cumin seeds until they begin to pop, then remove and put to one side. In the same pan, fry the potatoes until brown and crispy. Allow them to cool before adding the remaining ingredients. Toss well to mix all the flavours together.

Spicy peanut sambal

Makes 100g (4oz)

3–4 fresh hot green chillies, sliced into thin rounds
4 garlic cloves
25g (1oz) peanuts, fried or roasted
5 teaspoons Japanese soy sauce
4 teaspoons lime juice
4 teaspoons tamarind paste
4 teaspoons Fair Trade dark muscovado sugar
2 tablespoons water

An Indonesian sambal is a hotly spiced relish. It can be stirred into stews that lack lustre or, as in this recipe from Madhur Jaffrey, be used as a dip for raw vegetables or deep-fried potato chips. It is best to use a pestle and mortar if you have the time, but a spice grinder or blender will do a decent job.

Method

Grind all the ingredients together to a smooth sauce either with a mortar and pestle or in a blender or food processor. If the sauce seems too thick, add another tablespoon of water.

Fennel and watercress salad

Serves 4

- 1 red onion, thinly sliced
- 3 oranges, segmented and the juice reserved for the dressing
- 1 head of fennel, thinly sliced
- 100g (4oz) Fair Trade brazil nuts
- 1 tablespoon small capers
- 1 bunch of watercress, stalks removed

For the orange dressing
- 2 teaspoons Dijon mustard
- reserved juice of segmented oranges
- grated zest of 1 orange
- 120ml (4fl oz) olive oil
- salt and Fair Trade ground black pepper

Method

To make the dressing, use a small whisk to beat the mustard with the orange juice, then beat in the orange zest and olive oil and season with salt and pepper. Mix the red onion, orange segments and fennel with the dressing and allow to marinate for 30 minutes. When you are ready to eat, toss in the nuts, capers and watercress.

Fair Trade

Brazil nuts grown in the Peruvian rainforest are dried, graded, packed and exported by an alternative trading organization which enables pickers to buy boats, fuel and food.

Red cabbage coleslaw

Serves 4-6

350g (12oz) red cabbage, grated

100g (4oz) carrots, grated

1 onion, diced

2 small English apples (such as Cox's or Russett's), grated

50g (2oz) Fair Trade walnuts, crushed

50g (2oz) Fair Trade raisins

1 teaspoon celery seeds (optional)

For the dressing

2 teaspoons plain flour

2 teaspoons Fair Trade golden caster sugar

1 teaspoon mustard powder

1 teaspoon salt

Fair Trade chilli powder to taste

2 tablespoons wine vinegar

2 teaspoons butter

1 egg yolk

4-6 tablespoons double cream

This coleslaw dressing is Margaret Costa's recipe and the coleslaw is made with red cabbage instead of the usual white.

Method

Place all the coleslaw ingredients in a bowl and toss together well.

To make the dressing, mix the flour, sugar, mustard, salt and chilli powder together, then blend in the vinegar. Cook in a heavy-based pan over a low heat, stirring until the mixture thickens. Let it cool a little, stir in the butter and the egg yolk and lastly the cream. Beat until really well blended. Pour over the vegetables and toss together well.

Michael Barry's coleslaw

Serves 6

450g (1lb) white cabbage
225g (8oz) carrots, coarsely grated
100g (4oz) spring onions, white and green parts, chopped
1 red apple, cored and finely chopped

For the dressing

120ml (4fl oz) olive oil
4 tablespoons grapeseed oil or mild vegetable oil
juice of 1 lemon
1 garlic clove, crushed
1 heaped tablespoon Fair Trade clear honey
1 teaspoon Dijon mustard
salt and Fair Trade ground black pepper

This coleslaw is a Michael Barry recipe. It has such a marvellous flavour and texture it is hard to believe it's good for you as well.

Method

Cut the cabbage into quarters, then cut out the thick core and finely shred the leaves with a sharp knife. Mix the cabbage, carrots, spring onions and apple together in a large bowl.

To make the dressing, simply process all the ingredients together in a blender or whisk them together in a separate bowl. Pour over the vegetables and toss until they are lightly coated. Leave the coleslaw in the fridge for a few hours before serving, to bring out all the flavours.

Fair Trade

Globally, enough food is produced to provide every person in the world with the food they need to stay healthy. The problem is that some people can't afford to buy it. Supporting Fair Trade is a practical way to help people living in poverty to earn enough to pay for basic necessities.

Nigerian parsley and kuli-kuli salad

Serves 2

For the kuli-kuli
- 350g (12oz) peanuts, roasted
- juice and grated zest of 1 lime
- 1 egg
- 500ml (17fl oz) sunflower oil for deep-frying

For the salad
- 1 red onion, thinly sliced
- 1 red pepper, thinly sliced
- 1 large bunch of fresh flatleaf parsley
- 4 tablespoons olive oil
- 2 tablespoons lime juice
- 1 teaspoon Fair Trade chilli powder

Peanuts are a staple food of Nigeria. This is a slightly Westernized version but is faithful to its origins. If you find that the patties break up when being deep-fried, then lightly flour them before giving them the plunge.

Method

In a food processor, whizz the peanuts until you have a rough paste. Then add the lime juice, zest and egg and whizz again until thoroughly mixed. Mould the paste into small patties 2.5mm (1in) round and 5mm (¼ in) thick. Bring the sunflower oil up to frying heat and fry the patties in batches of 3 or 4 for 30 seconds until they are golden on both sides.

Mix together the red onion, pepper and parsley. Make the dressing by whisking together the olive oil, lime juice and chilli powder. Pour this over the salad, add the warm patties and toss together gently.

Tarator sauce

Serves 4

2 slices of white bread, crusts removed
100g (4oz) Fair Trade walnuts, finely ground
150ml (5fl oz) olive oil
3–4 tablespoons wine vinegar
1–2 garlic cloves, crushed
salt and Fair Trade ground black pepper

Tarator sauce is of Turkish origin. This recipe can be found in Jane Grigson's *The Fish Book* and gives just a glimpse of her great innovation and strength in matching flavours. She suggests serving the sauce with bass or bream but it is best enlivening slightly plainer fish such as cod. If you wish to experiment you can easily substitute hazelnuts, almonds or pine kernels for the walnuts.

Method

Dip the bread in the water and squeeze it dry. Crumble roughly and add to the nuts. Gradually mix in the olive oil, beating all the time, then add the vinegar and garlic. Season with salt and pepper. The simplest way is to put all the ingredients, except the salt and pepper, into the liquidizer and process at top speed until you have a smooth sauce. Finally, season to taste.

Desserts

Creamy orange bananas

Serves 4

50g (2oz) butter

4 medium semi-ripe bananas, peeled and halved lengthways

50g (2oz) Fair Trade demerara sugar

1 tablespoon dark rum

2 tablespoons orange juice

8 cardamom pods

1 teaspoon Fair Trade ground cinnamon

120ml (4fl oz) double cream

This dish needs you to stand over it, so have all the ingredients to hand. It should only take 10 minutes. You do not eat the whole cardamom.

Method

In a frying pan large enough to hold the bananas, melt the butter, being careful not to burn it. Place the bananas in the browning butter. As the undersides take on colour, turn the bananas and sprinkle on the sugar. Watch carefully as the dish cooks very quickly; you want the sugar the colour of caramel. When the sugar is golden, sprinkle in the rum. It will flame, but don't worry. Boil to reduce to a syrup, then add the orange juice and spices. Reduce again to a syrup, then pour in the cream. Allow the cream to come to a boil, then remove from the heat. Place the bananas on a plate and smother with the sauce.

Flambéed bananas with kumquat marmalade sauce

Serves 4

50g (2oz) butter
1 tablespoon sunflower or vegetable oil
4 bananas
3 tablespoons Fair Trade dark muscovado sugar
2 tablespoons brandy or Grand Marnier
juice of 1 orange
juice of 1 lime
½ jar Fair Trade Swazi Kitchen kumquat marmalade

This is a recipe contributed by Sophie Grigson. The tartness of the kumquat marmalade offsets the sweetness of the fried caramelized bananas perfectly. It is a dramatically quick pudding to make, and needs nothing more than a puddle of cream to finish it off.

Method

Melt the butter and oil in a frying pan over a moderate heat. While it heats up, peel the bananas and cut each one into three, slicing diagonally to make them look a little prettier. As soon as the butter is foaming, add the bananas. Fry, turning occasionally, until patched with brown. Sprinkle with the sugar and turn gently. Now add the brandy or Grand Marnier, warm through for a minute or so, then tilt the pan towards the flame if you cook on gas, so that the juices catch light. If your heat source is electric, light with a match held at arm's length. Once the flame dies down, lift the bananas into a warm serving dish and keep warm. Add the orange and lime juices and the marmalade. Stir together, then bring up to the boil and cook down hard until reduced by about half. Spoon over the bananas and serve with double cream.

Fair Trade

The Eswatini Swazi Kitchen in Swaziland realized that a lot of mangoes, kumquats and oranges were going to waste because they weren't able to export them as fresh fruit. With the help of a Fair Trade organization, they now produce jams, marmalades and sauces.

Baked figs with mascarpone and walnuts

Serves 4

12 ripe figs
50g (2oz) Fair Trade walnuts, coarsely chopped
3 tablespoons Fair Trade wild blossom honey
2 tablespoons Marsala or medium sherry
100g (4oz) mascarpone

Figs are often considered to be the most lush and meaty of all fruits. They are in their peak in late autumn and are swollen with the goodness of long summers. The majority of figs sold in Britain are grown in southern Europe and certainly add a touch of colour and flavour to the fruit bowl. This particular recipe comes from Nigel Slater's book, *Real Good Food,* and is characteristically rich and delicious.

Fair Trade

Honeys from Zambia are collected by traditional bee-keepers in an area which is sparsely populated and covered in woodland where bee-keeping is one of the few sources of income.

Method

Preheat the oven to 200°C/400°F/Gas 6. Cut a cross in the top of each fig and gently push the sides to an open hollow. Toast the walnuts under a hot grill until fragrant but barely coloured. Rub off the skins that have come loose. You do not have to be too pernickety about this. Mix the broken nuts with the honey, Marsala or sherry and mascarpone and carefully fill the figs with this mixture. Bake in the oven for about 15–20 minutes until bubbly. Serve warm.

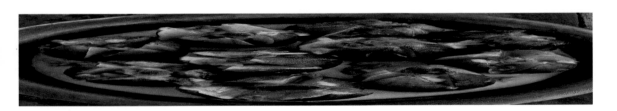

Baked apples stuffed with almonds

Serves 8

6 tablespoons Fair Trade clear organic honey

2 drops of vanilla essence

2 teaspoons Fair Trade ground cinnamon

100g (4oz) Fair Trade organic sultanas, soaked overnight in
   120ml (4fl oz) calvados

100g (4oz) Fair Trade almonds, chopped

100g (4oz) blackberries or any other dark berry

8 large Bramley cooking apples

75g (3oz) butter

Baked apples are found both in Middle Eastern and English cookery. The slight tartness of the apples offsets a rich and sweet filling.

Fair Trade

Honey from North Western Bee Products, Zambia, is produced in forests which are still in their natural state. NWBP has also been successful in marketing beeswax for use in candles and lip balm.

Method

Preheat the oven to 180°C/350°F/Gas 4. Mash together the honey, vanilla, cinnamon, sultanas, almonds and blackberries. Core the apples without cutting right through, and place them on a baking tray. Fill the centre of each apple with the blackberry mixture and top each one with a teaspoon of butter. Bake in the oven for 20–25 minutes until the apples are soft. Serve hot with cream, crème fraîche or, best of all, yoghurt.

Brunne

Serves 4

- **750ml (1¼ pints) milk**
- **6 aniseeds**
- **½ teaspoon Fair Trade ground cinnamon**
- **5 cloves**
- **200g (7oz) millet, washed**
- **2 tablespoons Fair Trade dark muscovado sugar**
- **1 tablespoon Fair Trade desiccated coconut**
- **1 tablespoon Fair Trade crushed mixed nuts**
- **1 tablespoon Fair Trade raisins**

This South American dish is basically a millet cream pudding. It is made following the same principle as an English rice pudding or an Italian polenta pudding. Millet on its own is a pretty bland affair so do serve it with bowls of the recommended garnishes.

Method

Pour the milk into a pan and add the aniseeds, cinnamon and cloves. Bring to the boil, then add the millet. Reduce the heat and simmer gently for 20 minutes. It is really important to stir the milk regularly otherwise it will stick and burn and be revolting. Discard the aniseeds and cloves. Transfer to a food processor and process the millet into a thick cream. You can serve it hot or cold with the sugar, coconut, nuts and raisins.

Fruit compote

Serves 6

100g (4oz) Fair Trade raisins
100g (4oz) dried dates
50g (2oz) dried fruit salad
50g (2oz) dried figs
1 teaspoon ground mixed spice
1 teaspoon Fair Trade ground cinnamon
1 teaspoon juniper berries, crushed
grated zest and segments of 2 oranges
300ml (10fl oz) Fair Trade cold Assam or Earl Grey tea

A rich and colourful compote, you can garnish the fruit with mint leaves as you can see in the photograph on page 102.

Method

Mix all the ingredients except the orange segments in a bowl and pour over the tea. Cover and leave in a cool place for 24 hours. When ready to serve, mix in the orange segments and serve on its own or with the Christmas Ricotta Soufflé (see page 103).

Fair Trade

Fair Trade shows that there really is an alternative to the mainstream trade which has caused so many problems. 'Trade has the power to create opportunities and support livelihoods; and it has the power to destroy them ...'

Sweet potato pie

Serves 4

- 250g (9oz) ready-made shortcrust pastry
- 225g (8oz) peeled, boiled sweet potato
- 225g (8oz) plain flour
- 75g (3oz) butter, melted
- 75g (3oz) Fair Trade dark muscovado sugar
- 175ml (6fl oz) single cream
- 2 large eggs
- 1/2 teaspoon Fair Trade grated nutmeg
- 1 teaspoon Fair Trade ground cinnamon
- 3 tablespoons brandy
- a good pinch of salt
- 75g (3oz) Fair Trade walnuts, coarsely chopped

Sweet potato pie is an adaptation of the good old American pumpkin pie. This recipe is taken from Jane Grigson's *The Vegetable Book*. She suggests serving it cold with plenty of whipped cream. It can be equally tasty served warmed up with vanilla ice cream and maple syrup. In for a penny, in for a pound!

Method

Preheat the oven to 200°C/400°F/Gas 6 and grease a 25cm (10in) loose-bottomed tart tin. Roll out the shortcrust pastry to about 5cm (2in) thick and line the tart tin with the pastry.

Sieve the sweet potato into a large bowl and beat in all the remaining ingredients, in the order given, except for the walnuts. Add a third of the walnuts to the sweet potato mixture. Pour this into the pastry case and arrange the remaining walnuts around the edge of the pie. They may sink in slightly but don't worry about this. Bake in the oven for about 40–45 minutes until the filling has risen and set. Test with a warm metal knife or skewer, as you would a baked custard, and when it comes out clean, remove the pie from the oven.

Pears baked with honey

Serves 8

4 pears
4 cloves
4 cardamom seeds, crushed
a pinch of Fair Trade ground cinnamon
a pinch of Fair Trade golden caster sugar
4 tablespoons Fair Trade Mexican clear honey
300ml (10fl oz) boiling water

Fair Trade

Mexican set honey is disadvantaged by a 25 per cent import duty, but despite this, Fair Trade still helps its producers to find the honey a much-needed place in the world market.

This is a recipe from Brian Turner which he has cooked on television on his morning cookery slot. It a cleverly spiced pudding that might otherwise be too sweet. Do take note of his instruction to baste the pears regularly, as the honey does burn very easily.

Method

Preheat the oven to 200°C/400°F/Gas 6. Peel the pears and core them from underneath, leaving the stalks on. Stick a clove in each of the pears and lay them on their sides in an ovenproof dish. Scatter the broken cardamom seeds over the pears and sprinkle with cinnamon. Dissolve the sugar and honey in the water, bring to the boil and boil for 2 minutes. Pour the syrup over the pears and bake in the oven for 1 hour until tender. Turn the pears occasionally and baste frequently. Serve warm with cream and pour a little more syrup over the top to finish.

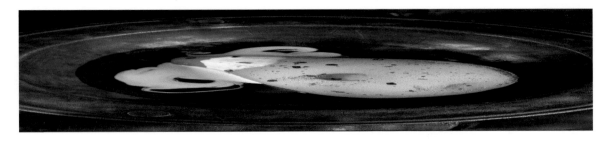

Praline chocolate terrine

Serves 12

For the compote

> 900g (2lb) red fruit, such as strawberries, raspberries, cherries
>
> Fair Trade golden caster sugar for sprinkling
>
> Kirsch to taste

For the chocolate cake mix

> 225g (8oz) Fair Trade Maya Gold dark chocolate
>
> 2 tablespoons Fair Trade strong black instant coffee
>
> 6 eggs, separated
>
> 100g (4oz) Fair Trade golden caster sugar

For the ganache

> 450g (1lb) Fair Trade praline chocolate, broken up
>
> 500ml (17fl oz) double cream

Winter is a time when the only consolations are indulgences. This is a classic example – a wonderfully rich and tempting dessert.

Method

To make the compote, prepare the fruit as necessary, then place in a shallow bowl. Sprinkle with a little sugar and Kirsch. Mix gently, cover and leave to stand for several hours, stirring occasionally.

Preheat the oven to 200°C/400°F/Gas 6 and line a 23cm (9in) square cake tin with a long strip of baking parchment to cover the base. To make the cake mix, melt the chocolate into the coffee in a heatproof bowl set over a pan of gently simmering water. Remove from the heat and whisk in the egg yolks and sugar. In a separate bowl, whisk the egg whites until they form stiff peaks. Using a wooden spoon, gently fold the stiff whites into the chocolate, trying not to knock the air out of the whites. Pour the cake mix into the loaf tin and bake in the oven for 15–20 minutes. The cake mix should just be beginning to darken on top and you should be able to pull a metal skewer cleanly out of the centre of the cake. Allow to cool before turning out and cutting into 3 strips, each one 23×7.5cm (9×3in).

To make the ganache, simply melt the chocolate into the cream in a pan over a medium heat, stirring all the time.

To assemble the terrine, line the bottom of a 23×7.5cm (9×3in) loaf tin with baking parchment. Then beginning with the ganache, alternate equal layers of the ganache and the cake strips, ending with a layer of ganache. Tap the tin to encourage the ganache to fall down the edges of the cake. Chill in the fridge for several hours until set. To serve, slip a knife around the sides of the terrine and turn it out. Cut into slices and arrange on a serving plate with the red fruit compote alongside. Serve with extra cream if liked.

Fair Trade

Launched in 1994, Maya Gold chocolate was the first commercial product to be awarded the Fairtrade Mark.

Pears in wine syrup

Serves 4

300ml (10fl oz) fruity red wine
100g (4oz) Fair Trade dark muscovado sugar
½ teaspoon Fair Trade ground cinnamon
1 teaspoon Fair Trade ground ginger
4 cloves
1 tablespoon quince or redcurrant jelly (optional)
1 orange
4 pears

Fair Trade

Fair Trade helps producers to export their products, but it may also help them to find new local markets. In Jamaica some big hotels have joined an 'adopt-a-farmer' scheme, entering into contract with local farmers.

This is an old English recipe dating back to Tudor times. It is believed that cooks of that time heavily spiced their foods to hide poor-quality produce. This may be true, but it is also the case that because spices were so expensive, using them to excess was a sign of wealth. In modern times with fresh produce and spices readily available, the British enjoy these recipes purely because they love rich, spicy and sweet puddings.

Method

Place the wine, sugar, spices and jelly, if using, in a heavy-based pan large enough to fit the pears and bring to the boil. Meanwhile, grate the zest and squeeze the juice from the orange and peel and core the pears, leaving them whole. Discard the orange pulp and place the juice and zest in the pan. When the sugar has dissolved, turn down the heat to a gentle simmer. Place the whole pears in the syrup and cover with a lid. Allow to simmer for 25–30 minutes, basting the pears with the syrup every so often. When they are tender but still holding their shape, remove them from the pan, place on a serving plate and keep warm. Bring the liquid to the boil and boil rapidly until reduced to a syrup. Pour over the pears.

Chocolate fondue

Serves 8

400g (14oz) Fair Trade nut chocolate
175ml (6fl oz) double cream
120ml (4fl oz) crème fraîche
2 tablespoons brandy

Method

Put chocolate, cream and crème fraîche into a heatproof bowl and place the bowl over a pan of boiling water. Heat gently, stirring all the time, until the chocolate melts. Stir in the brandy and leave the bowl over the hot water to keep warm until ready to serve. Serve with a selection of diced fruits to dip into the chocolate.

Praline

Serves 6

225g (8oz) Fair Trade almonds, blanched
175g (6oz) Fair Trade hazelnuts
450g (1lb) Fair Trade golden caster sugar

Method

Place the nuts and sugar in a heavy-based pan over a low heat. Gently turn the nuts with the melting sugar until the sugar turns a golden caramel and the nuts are toasted and coated with the sugar. Turn on to a cold work surface (marble, if you have it, or greased parchment paper). Allow to cool and set. This is wonderful just broken into pieces and sprinkled over ice cream and sorbets.

Fair Trade

Buying Fair Trade products doesn't necessarily mean you have to pay more. Fair Trade simply cuts out some of the middle men and this means that people who produce the food get a bigger percentage of the price you pay.

Christmas ricotta soufflés
Serves 6

sunflower oil for greasing
2 tablespoons Fair Trade golden caster sugar for dusting
400g (14oz) ricotta
grated zest of 3 lemons
3 tablespoons Fair Trade demerara sugar
1 tablespoon Fair Trade honey with orange juice
4 egg whites

These soufflés were created especially for vegetarians as an alternative to Christmas pudding and cake which are normally made with animal suet. But they do stand in their own right as a delicious light pudding for any time of the year. The use of ricotta in a pudding comes from Italian cooking and it makes an excellent alternative to cream. This dish goes very well with Fruit Compote (see page 94).

Method

Preheat the oven to 200°C/400°F/Gas 6. Lightly grease 6 individual ramekins and sprinkle each one with caster sugar. Place the ricotta in a bowl and add the lemon zest. Using a wooden spoon, beat in the sugar and honey until you have a creamy consistency. In a separate clean, dry bowl whisk the egg whites until they form stiff peaks. Carefully and lightly fold these into the lemon mixture until well combined. Divide the mixture evenly between the ramekins and cook in the top of the oven for 12–15 minutes until risen and slightly golden on top. Serve immediately with fresh fruit or fruit compote.

Fair Trade

'We do not see their lives when we buy something. If we did, we might choose to shop differently.'

Chocolate chip ice cream

Serves 10

350g (12oz) Fair Trade plain chocolate, chopped
250ml (8fl oz) milk
250ml (8fl oz) double cream
1/2 vanilla pod, split
4 egg yolks
25g (1oz) Fair Trade golden caster sugar

Anton Mosimann is famed for his chocolate recipes, so his chocolate chip ice cream is hard to match. To make a perfect ice cream it is very important to stick rigidly to the recipe. It is well worth the discipline.

Method

Melt 250g (9oz) of the chocolate in a heatproof bowl set over a pan of gently simmering water. Heat the milk, double cream and vanilla pod together and bring to the boil. Whisk together the egg yolks and sugar until they start to go pale. Slowly whisk the boiling milk into the egg yolks, then return the mixture to the pan and cook over a low heat, stirring all the time, until the mixture coats the back of a spoon. Strain the custard into the melted chocolate and blend well, then leave to cool. Place in a mould or container and freeze for 2–3 hours. When thick and half frozen, take out, place in a blender and process to a smooth, cold mixture. Chop the remaining chocolate very finely and stir in. Return to the container and the freezer for a further 1–2 hours until frozen.

Tip

You can serve the ice cream layered, at the last minute, between home-made chocolate biscuits or waffles. Another idea is to cut out circles of chocolate. Melt Fair Trade Mascao plain or Fair Trade Maya Gold chocolate gently, (perhaps with a little orange liqueur) and then pour it on to a cool work surface (or a piece of marble). When the chocolate has cooled a little, mark with a round pastry cutter, then leave to set completely. Remove the circles carefully and serve with the ice cream.

Raspberry ice cream

Serves 12

175ml (6fl oz) raspberry purée made from 275g (10oz)
   blended raspberries
250ml (8fl oz) double cream or thick plain yoghurt
1 tablespoon lemon juice
4 tablespoons Fair Trade clear honey
a pinch of salt
2 egg whites

This is a cheats ice cream, but the result is still delicious. To give it a creamier consistency, you may want to whisk the ice cream 2 or 3 times more after adding the whites just to stop ice crystals forming. But this is just for the perfectionists. It it is well worth trying this recipe with yoghurt rather than cream. If so, you may want to add another spoonful of honey.

Method

In a bowl, mix the raspberry purée with the cream or yoghurt. Thoroughly mix in the lemon juice, honey and salt. Turn the mixture into a shallow freezer tray and freeze until semi-frozen. This will take about 6 hours. Remove from the freezer and turn into a bowl. Beat until smooth, breaking down the ice crystals. Whisk the egg whites until stiff, then fold into the raspberry mixture. Return to the freezer for 4 hours until firm.

Apple strudel

Serves 6

For the pastry
- 250g (9oz) plain flour
- 1 egg
- 1 tablespoon olive oil
- 50ml (2fl oz) cold water
- 175g (6oz) butter, melted
- icing sugar for dusting

For the filling
- 100g (4oz) Fair Trade demerara sugar
- 1/2 teaspoon Fair Trade ground cinnamon
- 1/2 teaspoon Fair Trade ground ginger
- 120ml (4fl oz) water
- 100g (4oz) Fair Trade organic sultanas
- 3 large or 4 medium–sized cooking apples, peeled, cored and finely chopped
- 1 teaspoon lemon juice

Strudel is a traditional German pudding. The pastry in this dish is very important. It needs to have some elasticity to allow it to be rolled to paper thinness, and rolling the strudel on top of a floured cloth will help stop the pastry from tearing. Make sure your hands are cold before you start kneading the pastry.

Method

To make the pastry, sift the flour into a mixing bowl. Add the egg and oil, then pour in the water while mixing with a wooden spoon. When combined, turn out the dough on to a floured board and knead with your hands for 5 minutes. Roll the dough into a ball, cover with a damp cloth and allow to rest for at least 30 minutes in a warm place.

To make the filling, mix the sugar and spices in a pan. Gradually blend in the cold water followed by the sultanas, apple and lemon juice. Bring to the boil and simmer for 3 minutes. Remove from heat and allow to cool.

Preheat the oven to 200°C/400°F/Gas 6 and generously grease a baking tray. Roll out the pastry on a floured cloth as thin as it will go. Then flour your hands, slip your palms under the dough and stretch it from the centre until the dough is paper thin. Brush the top side of the dough with melted butter. Spread the cold filling mixture carefully over half of the pastry base, leaving a 5cm (2in) border. Fold in the border sides of the pastry over the filling and slowly gathering the cloth, roll up the pastry, turning and pulling as you go. Brush the outside of the strudel with the remaining butter and place on the baking tray. Bake in the oven for 30–35 minutes until golden. Remove from the oven and leave to cool before dusting the strudel with icing sugar.

Pecan nut torte

Serves 8

75g (3oz) butter
75g (3oz) Fair Trade golden caster sugar
1 egg
100g (4oz) Fair Trade pecans, ground
150g (5oz) plain flour
3–4 tablespoons Fair Trade mango or guava extra jam
icing sugar for dusting

This is a cake from Rose Elliot which is ideal for a late tea on a winter's day.
Try it with a pot of Fair Trade tea.

Method

Preheat the oven to 180°C/350°F/Gas 4 and grease an 18cm (7in) sandwich
tin. In a mixing bowl, cream the butter with the sugar until light and fluffy.
Beat in the egg. Stir in the ground pecans, then mix in sufficient flour to
give a fairly soft dough (not as firm as a pastry dough). Cut off a small
amount and set aside for the lattice. Shape the rest of the dough into a round
and place in the sandwich tin. Spread with the jam. Roll out the remaining
dough and cut into strips. Arrange in a lattice pattern over the jam. Bake in
the oven for about 20 minutes until the lattice topping is crisp and golden
brown. Sprinkle with icing sugar while still hot. Allow to cool before serving
with yoghurt, cream or ice cream.

Mango jelly

Serves 6

175g (6oz) Fair Trade sun-dried mango
50g (2oz) Fair Trade golden caster sugar
1 teaspoon Fair Trade ground cinnamon
finely shredded zest of 1/2 orange
juice of 1 orange
juice of 1 lime
1 tablespoon powdered gelatine

This is a relatively sweet jelly. If you want a slightly tarter flavour, add the juice from another lime.

Method

Fair Trade

Fair Trade gives people who have faced many difficulties in their lives a chance to reach their potential. 'People are like plants: they bow down and rise up again.' (Proverb from Madagascar.)

Soak the mangoes in 600ml (1 pint) cold water for 6 hours. Pour the fruit and water into a pan, adding the sugar, cinnamon and orange zest. Bring to the boil, then simmer gently for 20 minutes. Fit a sieve over a measuring jug, pour in the fruit and leave to drain. Add the orange and lime juice to the jug and enough cold water to make 600ml (1 pint) of liquid. Put 3 tablespoons of the liquid into a bowl and sprinkle the gelatine on to the liquid. When the liquid has been absorbed, place the bowl over boiling water and dissolve the gelatine. When transparent, stir into the remaining liquid. Roughly chop the fruit and arrange in the bottom of a 1 litre (1¾ pint) jelly mould. Pour in the liquid and leave in a cold place to cool and set.

Bolivian banana surprise

Serves 4

- 200g (7oz) Fair Trade banana chips
- 300ml (10fl oz) medium-sweet sherry
- 20 sponge finger biscuits
- 400g (14oz) mascarpone
- 3–4 tablespoons Greek yoghurt
- 4 egg yolks, well beaten
- 100g (4oz) Fair Trade milk chocolate, coarsely grated
- 3–4 tablespoons Fair Trade honey
- 3–4 tablespoons Fair Trade desiccated coconut

For the garnish
- candied orange peel or fresh orange slices
- Fair Trade cashew nuts, toasted and chopped

This is a recipe especially written for Oxfam by Valentina Harris. The layering of bananas, biscuits, cream and toppings is very attractive and if you cut down on the sherry, it goes down a treat with children.

Method

Soak the banana chips in the sherry for at least 4 hours, preferably overnight. Drain the bananas thoroughly and reserve the sherry. Dilute the sherry with enough water to make up 300ml (10fl oz). Purée the bananas in a food processor. Soak half the biscuits in the sherry and use to line 6 stemmed glasses. Reserve the rest of the sherry and the remaining biscuits.

Now beat the mascarpone and yoghurt with the egg yolks to make a thick cream. Add three-quarters of the grated chocolate, the honey and coconut. Spoon half of this cream over the soaked biscuits. Divide the puréed bananas between the glasses, placing them in a layer over the cream. Now soak the remaining biscuits and arrange a second layer of biscuits. Decorate the surface of each Bolivian banana surprise with the remaining chocolate, thin slices of candied orange peel or slices of fresh orange and a sprinkle of toasted cashews. Chill thoroughly until required.

Fair Trade

In Zambia's North-western Province, people live on very little money, growing most of their own needs. The income they get from selling wild honey to Fair Trade organizations pays for a few extras.

Pecan pie

Makes 24 squares

For the pastry
- 275g (10oz) plain flour
- a pinch of salt
- 50g (2oz) Fair Trade golden caster sugar
- 175g (6oz) cold butter
- grated zest of 1 lemon
- 1 small egg

For the topping
- 100g (4oz) butter, diced
- 4 tablespoons Fair Trade forest clear honey
- 25g (1oz) Fair Trade golden caster sugar
- 3 tablespoons double cream
- 150g (5oz) Fair Trade pecans, chopped
- 1/2 teaspoon vanilla essence

Method

To make the pastry, sift the flour with the salt into a mixing bowl and stir in the sugar. Rub the butter into the flour until you have a texture of breadcrumbs. Stir in the lemon zest, then mix in the egg and pull together into a soft dough. Roll into a ball, wrap in clingfilm and leave to rest in the fridge for 30 minutes.

Preheat the oven to 190°C/375°F/Gas 5 and butter a 20×30cm (8×10in) baking tin. With floured fingertips, press the pastry into the bottom of the tin. Prick all over with a fork and again leave to rest in the fridge for 30 minutes. Weigh down the pastry with greaseproof paper and baking beans and bake in the oven for 15 minutes. Remove the paper and beans.

To make the topping, melt the butter and honey in a pan. Add the sugar and stir until dissolved. Remove from the heat and stir in the cream, pecans and vanilla essence. Pour the mixture over the pastry and return it to the oven for a further 25 minutes. Allow to cool before turning out.

Cakes and Biscuits

Chocolate cake

Serves 12

- 175g (6oz) plain flour
- 3 tablespoons Fair Trade cocoa
- 1 teaspoon baking powder
- 1 teaspoon bicarbonate of soda
- 150g (5oz) Fair Trade golden caster sugar
- 1 tablespoon black treacle
- 2 eggs
- 150ml (5fl oz) vegetable oil
- 150ml (5fl oz) milk
- apricot jam, cream or butter icing to finish

This is another recipe from Michael Barry. He was one of the first celebrity television cooks to give publicity to Fair Trade products. He has a sweet tooth and is not afraid of sweetness. He has craftily varied the source of sugar in this recipe by adding black treacle.

Method

Preheat the oven to 160°C/325°F/Gas 3 and grease 2×18cm (7in) cake tins. Mix all the dry ingredients together in a food processor and whizz the ingredients until thoroughly blended. Add the liquid ingredients and process again, scraping the sides of the bowl until they are all thoroughly incorporated. If you do not have a processor, you can do this by hand. Pour the mixture into the tins and bake in the oven for 45 minutes. Cool and then sandwich with apricot jam, cream or butter icing as you choose.

Fair Trade

To show what Fair Trade means to them, farmers and factory workers producing cocoa in Alto Beni, Bolivia, have named their organization El Ceibo, after the tree that shelters their cocoa plants.

Chocolate, prune and almond cake

Makes 12 slices

350g (12oz) Fair Trade orange chocolate
200g (7oz) unsalted butter
75g (3oz) Fair Trade hazelnuts
75g (3oz) Fair Trade brazil nuts
75g (3oz) Fair Trade almonds, blanched
100g (4oz) soft prunes
2 eggs, lightly beaten

'The richest of all chocolate cakes, with the texture of a chocolate truffle.'
This is the introduction that Nigel Slater gives to this recipe in his book
Real Good Food. The cake should be served in thin slivers topped with
whipped cream or ice cream.

Method

Line a 20cm (8in) square cake tin. Melt 225g (8oz) of the chocolate and all
the butter together in a heavy-based pan over a low heat. Spread the nuts on
a grilling tray and toast under a hot grill till the skins begin to blister. Rub
the nuts with a cloth, discarding the skins, then return the nuts to the grill
until golden brown. When the chocolate is melted, remove from the heat and
stir in the nuts, prunes and eggs. Spoon the mixture into the lined cake tin
and leave to set in the fridge overnight.

When completely set, remove from the tin and peel off the paper. Melt
the remaining chocolate in a bowl over a pan of gently simmering water,
then pour the chocolate over the cake and return the cake to the fridge to
set. With a large heavy knife, cut the cake in half. Then cut each half into
6 slices, making 12 slices in total.

Honey spice cake

Serves 8

- 75g (3oz) Fair Trade clear organic set honey
- 250g (9oz) plain flour
- 1 teaspoon Fair Trade ground ginger
- 1 teaspoon Fair Trade ground cinnamon
- 1/2 teaspoon ground cloves
- 75g (3oz) Fair Trade golden caster sugar
- finely grated zest of 1 lemon
- finely grated zest of 1 orange
- 100g (4oz) butter
- 1 egg
- 1 teaspoon bicarbonate of soda
- 50g (2oz) Fair Trade dried apricots, blended to a paste

For the icing

- 100g (4oz) icing sugar, sifted
- 1 1/2 tablespoons lemon juice
- 1–2 tablespoons warm water

This is a tangy and fruity and very generously flavoured cake.

Method

Preheat the oven to 160°C/325°F/Gas 3 and lightly butter a 18cm (7in) square cake tin. Warm the honey in a bowl over a pan of gently simmering water. Sift the flour and spices into a mixing bowl, then add the sugar and fruit zest. Rub the butter into the flour until crumbly. Lightly mix in the egg and honey. In a separate small bowl, mix the bicarbonate of soda with 3 tablespoons of cold water until dissolved, then add to cake mix and beat well. Stir in the apricots and spread the mixture into the tin. Bake in the oven for about 30 minutes. Cool for 10 minutes in the tin before turning out.

To make the icing, sift the icing sugar into a bowl. Add the lemon juice and water and mix until well blended. Pour the icing over the cake. It will take a little while to set.

Fair Trade

Cinnamon, chilli, ginger, black and white pepper, turmeric and cloves are grown and ground in South India and imported for packing in England.

Gingerbread cake

Serves 4

450g (1lb) plain flour
3/4 tablespoon Fair Trade ground ginger
1 teaspoon baking powder
1 teaspoon bicarbonate of soda
a pinch of salt
25g (1oz) Fair Trade demerara sugar
100g (4oz) unsalted butter
100g (4oz) black treacle
100g (4oz) golden syrup
1 egg
150ml (5fl oz) milk

Gary Rhodes' gingerbread cake can be served as a warm pudding or simply as a cold cake. It eats really well with clotted cream.

Method

Preheat the oven to 180°C/350°F/Gas 4 and grease and line a 900g (2lb) loaf tin. Mix together the flour, ginger, baking powder, bicarbonate of soda and salt in a bowl. Warm the sugar, butter, treacle and golden syrup together in a pan. Beat the egg into the milk, then mix in all the ingredients in the bowl. Pour the mixture into the prepared tin and spread it out evenly. Simply bake in the oven for 1¼ hours. Remove from the tin and leave to stand for a few minutes before serving warm or just leave to cool.

Rich fruit cake

Serves 12

225g (8oz) Fair Trade organic sultanas

225g (8oz) Fair Trade raisins

225g (8oz) currants

100g (4oz) glacé cherries, halved

100g (4oz) Fair Trade almonds, chopped

250ml (8fl oz) brandy

120ml (4fl oz) orange juice

225g (8oz) Fair Trade dark muscovado sugar

225g (8oz) butter

4 eggs, lightly beaten

225g (8oz) plain flour

50g (2oz) self-raising flour

1 teaspoon mixed spice

1/2 teaspoon Fair Trade grated nutmeg

1 teaspoon Fair Trade ground cinnamon

Method

Soak the dried fruit, cherries and almonds in the brandy and orange juice overnight.

Preheat the oven to 140°C/275°F/Gas 1 and grease and line a 23cm (9in) round cake tin. Beat the sugar and butter together, then gradually add the eggs. Sift the flours and spices into the mixture and blend in. Mix in the fruit and brandy. Tip the mixture into the tin and bake in the centre of the oven for 3½–4 hours. Test with a skewer inserted in the middle of the cake. Leave it for 5 seconds, and if it comes out clean the cake is cooked. Leave to cool in the tin and then turn out.

For decoration, glaze the cake with brandy and Fair Trade apricot jam and decorate with Fair Trade pecans, walnuts, dried apricots and dried dates.

Christmas cake

Serves 6-10

225g (8oz) Fair Trade organic sultanas
175g (6oz) currants
100g (4oz) glacé cherries, rinsed and dried
125-250g (2-4oz) brandy
225g (8oz) butter, diced
225g (8oz) Fair Trade golden caster sugar
4 eggs
225g (8oz) plain flour
1 teaspoon mixed spice
1/2 teaspoon baking powder
a pinch of salt
50g (2oz) Fair Trade almonds or pecans, roughly chopped

For the icing

450g (1lb) icing sugar
1 egg white
juice of 1 lemon

Paul and Jeanne Rankin have produced this old-fashioned Christmas cake. It is moist and full of flavour. The liquor and the icing will ensure that the cake will mature nicely for up to 2 months.

Method

Preheat the oven to 110°C/225°F/Gas ¼ and grease a 20cm (8in) cake tin. Soak the fruit overnight in half the brandy. Cream the butter and the sugar together for about 5 minutes until light and fluffy. Slowly add the eggs, one by one, beating well after each addition. Sift all the dry ingredients together. Fold into the butter, sugar and egg mixture by hand. Lastly, fold in the fruit, with any juices, and the nuts.

Pour the batter into the tin and bake in the centre of the oven for about 2½-3 hours, or perhaps a little longer. If the top starts to brown you can simply cover it with greaseproof paper or foil. The cake is done when a skewer inserted in the centre comes out clean and the sides of the cake are pulling away from the sides of the tin. Remove from the oven and leave to cool for 10 minutes before turning out on to a wire rack. Using a skewer, or a cocktail stick, poke holes all over the top of the cake and pour over the rest of the brandy. The cake will absorb all of it. The cake is best eaten if made a week in advance and stored in a plastic container. The flavours will blend and develop during that time.

To make the icing, mix all the ingredients together until smooth and shiny. If you prefer to have a layer of marzipan on the cake, roll it out and shape it over the cake, then ice with the icing and decorate as desired.

Swahili buns

Makes 32 buns

500g (1lb 2oz) plain white flour
50g (2oz) Fair Trade golden caster sugar
2 tablespoons ghee or clarified butter
1 teaspoon dried yeast diluted in a little warm water
200ml (7fl oz) tinned coconut milk
½ teaspoon ground cardamom
½ teaspoon Fair Trade ground cinnamon
oil for deep-frying

Mahamri are sweet buns that in Africa would be eaten with a main meal. If you find them a little too sweet to serve with a meal, they make a tasty quick snack or a late lunch served with chutney and a tomato salad.

Method

Thoroughly knead all the ingredients except the frying oil to form a dough. Knead until the dough is smooth. Divide into 8 balls. Roll each ball into a 15cm (6in) circle and cut into quarters. Place on a floured board, cover with a damp cloth and leave to prove in a warm room for about 2 hours or until the dough has risen and become light. Heat the frying oil and deep-fry on both sides for about 5 minutes until light brown.

Date and walnut bread

Serves 4

300ml (10fl oz) milk
50g (2oz) butter
75g (3oz) black treacle
350g (12oz) plain flour
3 teaspoons baking powder
1/2 teaspoon salt
1/2 teaspoon bicarbonate of soda
75g (3oz) Fair Trade dark muscovado sugar
100g (4oz) dried dates, coarsely chopped
50g (2oz) Fair Trade walnuts, coarsely chopped

Fair Trade

Fair Trade organizations pay producers directly ... which means that the producers don't need to rely on money lenders who often charge extortionate interest rates on loans and take advantage of their difficult circumstances.

This a sticky and fruity tea cake which comes from a book written by Margaret Costa called *Four Seasons Cookery Book*. This has just been brought back into print after an absence of 26 years. A sign of a book being a classic is whether its recipes stand the test of time. This recipe is as young and lively as it was 20 years ago.

Method

Preheat the oven to 160°C/325°F/Gas 3 and grease and flour a 450g (1lb) loaf tin. Warm the milk with the butter and treacle until the butter has just melted. Sift the dry ingredients together and stir in the sugar. Mix in the chopped dates and nuts. Stir in the liquid, mix to a fairly smooth batter and turn out into the loaf tin. Smooth the top and bake in the oven for 1 hour or a little longer until a skewer inserted in the centre comes out clean.

Gingernuts

Makes 24

100g (4oz) self-raising flour
1 teaspoon Fair Trade ground ginger
1 teaspoon bicarbonate of soda
50g (2oz) Fair Trade dark muscovado sugar
50g (2oz) butter, diced
2 tablespoons golden syrup

This recipe makes very light and fluffy biscuits. If you prefer a more solid crunch, then use half self-raising flour to half plain flour. If you are feeling particularly racy, then add 1 teaspoon of finely chopped pickled ginger when you add the golden syrup.

Method

Preheat the oven to 190°C/375°F/Gas 5 and grease 2 baking sheets. Sift the flour, ginger and the bicarbonate of soda into a mixing bowl. Measure in the sugar and the butter and rub together with the tips of your fingers. When you have a breadcrumb consistency, pour in the syrup and stir into a paste using a wooden spoon and persistence; the mixture will be quite stiff. Roll out the dough and cut out about 24 biscuits with a pastry cutter. Place on the baking sheets with a little space between each one. Flatten slightly with a fork. Bake in the oven for 15–20 minutes until the biscuits have darkened in colour. Allow to cool and set slightly before transferring to a wire rack to finish cooling.

Fair Trade

'Our main aim is to show people ... that we as small-scale producers in the Third World exist, and we are working together for our communities to try to bring about improvements.'

Orange and chocolate biscuits

Makes 30

150g (5oz) butter
175g (6oz) Fair Trade golden caster sugar
175g (6oz) plain flour
2 teaspoons baking powder
75g (3oz) Fair Trade Maya Gold dark chocolate, chopped
grated zest of 2 oranges
1 tablespoon orange juice
extra Fair Trade golden caster sugar to decorate

These biscuits are great with vanilla ice cream. Keep a careful eye when you are cooking them. They need to be taken out when the biscuits are still soft. They will harden when out in the open.

Method

Preheat the oven to 180°C/350°F/Gas 4 and grease a baking sheet. Cream the butter and sugar together until they are pale and fluffy. Carefully mix in the flour and baking powder. Add the rest of the ingredients until you have a smooth, stiff paste. Roll out the paste 5mm–1cm (¼–½in) thick on a lightly floured working surface. Using a 5cm (2in) cutter, cut out the rounds and place on the baking sheet. Sprinkle the biscuits with a little additional sugar and bake in the oven for about 12–15 minutes until the biscuits begin to colour. Remove from the oven and leave to cool for at least 5 minutes to allow the biscuits to firm up before transferring to a cooling rack. Store in an airtight tin.

Drinks and Confectionery

Oxfam tea blend

2 parts Fair Trade Earl Grey tea
2 parts Fair Trade Assam loose tea
1 part Darjeeling tea

Method

Mix the tea leaves together and store in an airtight container.

Spiced Somalian tea

Serves 6

1 teaspoon Fair Trade ground cinnamon
seeds from 8 Fair Trade whole cardamom pods
6 cloves
2 Fair Trade black peppercorns
1.5 litres (2$\frac{1}{2}$ pints) cold water
$\frac{1}{2}$ teaspoon Fair Trade ground ginger
$\frac{1}{2}$ teaspoon Fair Trade grated nutmeg
75g (3oz) Fair Trade dark muscovado sugar
a pinch of leaf tea

By choosing Fair Trade tea you can help tea pickers to build new classrooms so that their children don't have to have lessons out in the monsoon rains.

Method

Grind together the cinnamon, cardamom seeds, cloves and peppercorns. Place the water in a pan and add the spices, ginger and nutmeg and bring to the boil. When the water is boiling, gradually stir in the sugar until dissolved. Remove from the heat and add the tea. Cover and allow to stand for 5 minutes. Strain the liquid into a jug and serve.

Tchai

Serves 4

In Mauritius, a co-operative of 500 tea producers lease their smallholding from the government and receive a guaranteed fair price for their tea.

1.2 litres (2 pints) milk

1.2 litres (2 pints) water

2 aniseeds

4 cloves

3 teaspoons Fair Trade ground cinnamon

2 Fair Trade teabags (preferably fruit-flavoured tea)

2 vanilla pods

1 teaspoon Fair Trade ground ginger

a small pinch of Fair Trade ground black pepper (optional)

Method

In a pan, mix all the ingredients together and bring to the boil. Turn down the heat and boil gently for about 2 minutes. Serve hot.

Hot chocolate toddy

Serves 2

75g (3oz) Fair Trade plain chocolate, chopped

400ml (14fl oz) hot milk

1 tablespoon Fair Trade dark muscovado sugar

1 egg

3 tablespoons brandy

Method

Place the chocolate, hot milk and sugar in a food processor and blend until the chocolate has melted and is well combined. Add the egg and the brandy and blend for 20 seconds. Pour into two heatproof glasses and serve.

Tanzanian summer tea

Serves 8

- 1.2 litres (2 pints) boiling water
- 6 Fair Trade Tanzanian teabags
- 2 tablespoons Fair Trade golden caster sugar
- 12 sprigs of fresh mint
- lots of ice
- 300ml (10fl oz) freshly squeezed orange juice, chilled
- juice of 1/2 lime
- juice of 1/2 orange
- 1/2 orange, sliced
- 1/2 lime, sliced

You can see this refreshing summer drink in the photograph on page 132 (right).

Method

Make the tea in a pot by pouring the boiling water over the teabags. Add the sugar and 6 sprigs of mint to the tea and allow to infuse for 20 minutes. Remove the teabags and leave the tea to cool. When cold, remove the mint leaves. Place lots of ice into an iced jug and pour in the cold tea, the orange and lime juice and the remaining mint. Add the sliced fruit, stir thoroughly and serve.

Fair Trade

'In the old days, we got a very bad price for our coffee crop. The traders got most of the profit. Now we get a better price because we have formed a co-operative and we control the marketing.'

Jamaican hot chocolate
Serves 2

25g (1oz) Fair Trade mocha chocolate, grated
300ml (10fl oz) Fair Trade hot black coffee
2 teaspoons Fair Trade demerara sugar
1 tablespoon dark rum
2 tablespoons whipped cream
extra grated Fair Trade plain chocolate, to decorate

Method

Place the chocolate, coffee and sugar in a food processor and process until blended. Add the rum and pour into two heatproof glasses. Top with whipped cream and sprinkle with grated chocolate. Serve immediately.

Fair Trade

'We produce coffee here for Fair Trade. We are careful to select only the best cherries … There is only one day when they are perfect. If it rains on that day, then they fall from the bushes and are lost. But it is a risk we are happy to take …'

Coffee calypso
Serves 1

2 tablespoons Tia Maria or other coffee-based liqueur
1 teaspoon Fair Trade palm sugar
120ml (4fl oz) Fair Trade hot coffee
2 tablespoons double cream
Fair Trade instant coffee granules to decorate

Method

Pour the liqueur into a heatproof glass and add the sugar and coffee. Stir well and slowly pour the cream over the back of a teaspoon into the glass so that it floats on top. Sprinkle with coffee granules and serve immediately.

Fair Trade

'The higher price we get when we sell to Cafédirect means that now I can afford more food for my family and send my children to school properly equipped with pens and notebooks for the first time.'

Left: Coffee calypso (left); Jamaican hot chocolate (middle); Tanzanian summer tea (right)

Strawberry and almond cup

Serves 2

90g (3¹/₂oz) Fair Trade almonds, blanched
100g (4oz) fresh or frozen strawberries
piece of vanilla pod or 2 drops vanilla essence
300ml (10fl oz) cold water
2 teaspoons Fair Trade clear organic honey
strawberry slices to garnish

Method

Place the almonds, strawberries and vanilla in a blender or food processor
with a little of the water and blend into a creamy purée. Add the rest of the
water and the honey and blend again. Pour into tall glasses, decorate with the
strawberry slices and serve at once.

Real hot chocolate

Serves 2

50g (2oz) praline chocolate, broken into pieces
300ml (10fl oz) milk

Method

Place the chocolate in a jug. Bring the milk to the boil in a pan. Pour about
a quarter of the milk on to the chocolate. Leave until the chocolate has
softened, then whisk until smooth. Return the remaining milk to the heat
and bring back to the boil. Pour this on to the chocolate mixture, whisking
continuously. Serve immediately.

Cinnamon chocolate

Add a teaspoon of Fair Trade ground cinnamon to the milk when bringing it to the boil. When poured into a glass, top with whipped cream and a sprinkling of Fair Trade cinnamon or cocoa.

Mocha

Dissolve 3 teaspoons of Fair Trade instant coffee in the hot milk while bringing it to the boil. Serve topped with whipped cream and Fair Trade chopped pecans sprinkled over the top.

Milk and almond drink
Serves 2

> **150g (5oz) Fair Trade almonds, blanched**
> **300ml (10fl oz) water**
> **6 fresh mint leaves**
> **450ml (15fl oz) very cold skimmed milk**
> **1 tablespoon Fair Trade golden caster sugar**

Fair Trade

Fair Trade chocolate is manufactured in Switzerland from organic cocoa beans grown by a group of 36 co-operatives in the lowlands of Bolivia.

This recipe is called *thandai* and comes from *Eastern Vegetarian Cooking* by Madhur Jaffrey. She has the ability to conjure up the atmosphere of the history of her dishes and tells many tales of her childhood. She describes this drink as a very cool and refreshing, summer drink which was sold out of terracotta pots throughout the plains of northern India. The drink is lightly spiced and sweetened with a subtle flavour of almonds.

Method

Soak the almonds in the water overnight, or for at least 5 hours; drain.

Place 4 mint leaves in a blender with 120ml (4fl oz) of the milk, the almonds and the sugar. Blend well, then pour in the rest of the milk. Pour into 2 glasses, garnish each one with a mint leaf and serve very cold. This can be made several hours ahead and stored, covered, in the fridge.

Icy chocolate milk

Makes 600ml (1 pint) syrup

Fair Trade

Oxfam's Fair Trade
cocoa grown in the
shade of palm trees in
the tropical region of
Ghana was voted 'best
cocoa' by a panel of
food experts, beating
cocoas which were as
much as ten times
more expensive.

250g (9oz) Fair Trade golden caster sugar
300ml (10fl oz) water
75g (3oz) Fair Trade cocoa
To serve
    milk
    crushed ice
    vanilla ice cream
    whipped cream
    Fair Trade cocoa to sprinkle

It is always handy to have back-up snacks in the fridge. You can make this
chocolate paste to keep in the fridge ready to be made into a delicious
chocolate drink whenever you are ready. The syrup makes an excellent
topping for ice cream too.

Method

Heat the sugar with the water in a pan until dissolved, then boil for 3
minutes, stirring occasionally. Whisk in the cocoa and continue whisking over
a moderate heat until smooth. Leave to cool and store in the fridge until
ready to serve.

For each serving, whisk together 250ml (8fl oz) of cold milk and 3
tablespoons of the chilled chocolate syrup. Pour into a chilled glass with a
little crushed ice. Float a scoop of ice cream on top with a little whipped
cream. Sprinkle with a little cocoa and serve immediately.

Mulled wine

Serves 6

1 bottle Chilean red wine

300ml (10fl oz) cold tea, made using 2 Fair Trade
   Assam tea bags

1 orange pierced with 10 cloves

1 teaspoon Fair Trade ground cinnamon

2 teaspoons Fair Trade ground ginger

100g (4oz) Fair Trade demerara sugar

Method

Gently heat all the ingredients together in a large pan until the mixture comes to the boil. Turn down the heat and simmer for 10 minutes. Serve in tall glasses with a teaspoon in to prevent the glass from cracking.

Quick chocolate truffles

Makes about 24

100g (4oz) Fair Trade Maya Gold dark chocolate

100g (4oz) unsalted butter

100g (4oz) icing sugar

2 teaspoons Fair Trade Cafédirect instant coffee

2 tablespoons Fair Trade cocoa

Helge Rubinstein created this delicious recipe.

Method

Melt the chocolate in a bowl over a pan of simmering water. Beat into the cooled melted chocolate the butter, sugar and the coffee. Chill the mixture in the fridge for 30 minutes until it has hardened sufficiently to be rolled into balls. Roll them in the cocoa and store in the fridge until ready to serve.

Fair Trade

'There are 4000 coffee producers in my organization, from different countries in Latin America and Africa. The small-scale producers are the ones that do most for the environment. They can't afford to buy the chemical products such as fertilizers, pesticides and insecticides that are needed for technical agriculture.'

More about
FAIR TRADE products

There are already some food products in major supermarket chains that you can identify from the labels as having been 'fairly traded' (in Britain these carry the Fairtrade Mark). In many countries there are alternative trading organizations offering a wide range of fairly traded foods from high street shops or by seasonal mail order. You can get more information from the addresses listed below:

Oxfam Trading Fair Trade foods and household products are available from the Oxfam Fair Trade Co. shops and many of the extensive chain of Oxfam shops in the United Kingdom and Ireland. Or order from Oxfam's mail order catalogue, available from Oxfam Trading, PO Box 72, Bicester, Oxon, OX6 7LT.

Traidcraft offers a wide range of fairly traded goods through independent retail outlets and local church groups. The range is also available by mail order from Traidcraft plc, Kingsway, Gateshead, NE11 0NE.

The Fairtrade Foundation was set up to promote fairer international trade in mainstream commercial markets. It has set criteria and standards in order to award a 'people friendly' stamp of approval – the Fairtrade Mark, which appears on products in Britain which have met the standards set by the Foundation.

Bridgehead is the trading organisation of Oxfam Canada. Their fairly traded goods are available in North America by mail order from Bridgehead, PO Box 1083, Station B, Willowdale, Ontario M2K 2P8, Canada.

The Irish Fair Trade Network produces a directory of outlets for fairly traded goods in Ireland. They can be contacted at Little Orchard House, Newpark, Kilkenny.

Oxfam Wereldwinkels and **Magasins du Monde** are networks of Fair Trade and information shops associated with Oxfam Belgium. For more information, contact Magasins du Monde Oxfam, rue Michiels 7a, 1180 Bruxelles, Belgium; and Oxfam Wereldwinkels vzw, Niewland 35-37, B-9000 Gent, Belgium.

CAA Trading supports the work of Community Aid Abroad/Oxfam in Australia with funds generated by ethical trading and by education work in Australia. Their mail order catalogue can be obtained from CAA Trading Pty Ltd, PO Box 184, Kilkenny, SA 5009, Australia.

Oxfam For information about Oxfam (United Kingdom and Ireland) or to learn more about Fair Trade, contact Oxfam, Supporter Information Unit, 274 Banbury Road, Oxford OX2 7DZ.

Credits

Spiced Fried Dahl by Malini Dissanayake, *Rose Elliot's Oxfam Vegetarian Cooking for Children* © Oxfam (Ebury Press, 1995)

Spinach and Walnut Omelette © Claudia Roden, *New Book of Middle Eastern Food* (Penguin Books Ltd, 1988)

South African Kebabs by Troth Wells, *The Spices of Life* © Troth Wells/New Internationalist (New Internationalist, 1994)

Fried Mussels with Garlic and Walnut Sauce by Sophie Grigson, *Travels à la Carte* © Sophie Grigson and William Black (Network Books, 1994)

Mackerel Baked in Tea © Sara Paston-Williams, *The National Trust Book of Fish Cookery* (National Trust Enterprises Ltd, 1988)

Spicy Salmon Tartare on Banana Chips © Antony Worrall Thompson

Noodles with Spiced Chicken Soup by Aung San Suu Kyi, *Recipes from Around the World* © Oxfam, 1983

Cashew Chilli Chicken © Ken Hom

Swaziland Turkey Goujons © Dudley Newbery

Yucatan-style Chicken © Elisabeth Lambert Ortiz, *Latin American Cookery* (Penguin Books Ltd, 1985)

Chicken with Green Curry, Mango, Lime and Coconut © Raymond Blanc, *Blanc Mange* (reproduced by permission of BBC Worldwide Ltd, 1994)

Marinated Chicken with Honey and Ginger Served with Sultana Salsa © Delia Smith, 1995 (reproduced by permission from *Sainsbury's The Magazine* published by New Crane Publishing Ltd)

Chicken with Squash, Pineapple and Chilli Sauce © Sophie Grigson

Lamb Biryani, *Recipes from Around the World* © Oxfam, 1983

Spiced Lamb, © Oxfam Wereldwinkels/Magasins du Monde (Oxfam in Belgium)

Tagine of Lamb or Mutton with Fruit and Almonds © Sophie Grigson, *Sophie Grigson's Meat Course* (Network Books, 1995)

Lamb Satay by Nicki Sissons, *Recipes from Around the World* © Oxfam, 1983

Ghanian Pumpkin © Ola Olaore, *Traditional African Cookery* (Foulsham, 1990)

Beef and Rice Omelette © Sri Owen, *The Rice Book* (Transworld Publishers Ltd, 1993)

Barbecued Fish with Dates by Tess Mallos, *The Complete Middle East Cookbook* © Charmaine Solomon (Grub Street, 1995)

Kedgeree © Rick Stein, *Rick Stein's Taste of the Sea* (BBC Worldwide, 1995)

Warm Thai Mussel Salad with Mint © Jill Dupleix

Nasi Goreng by Roberta Jordan, *Rose Elliot's Oxfam Vegetarian Cooking for Children* © Oxfam (Ebury Press, 1995)

Leek and Almond Filo Pie by Don Hacker, *Rose Elliot's Oxfam Vegetarian Cooking for Children* © Oxfam (Ebury Press, 1995)

Millet Gratin © Oxfam Wereldwinkels/Magasins du Monde (Oxfam in Belgium)

Fruit Curry © Rose Elliot

Millet Balls © Oxfam Wereldwinkels/Magasins du Monde (Oxfam in Belgium)

Rhubarb Khoresh © Sri Owen, *The Rice Book* (Transworld Publishers Ltd, 1993)

Spiced Mixed Vegetables with Coconut © Madhur Jaffrey, *Eastern Vegetarian Cooking* (Jonathan Cape, 1992)

Gujarati-style Yoghurt with Potatoes © Lindsey Bareham, *In Praise of the Potato* (Penguin Books Ltd, 1991)

Spicy Peanut Sambal © Madhur Jaffrey, *Eastern Vegetarian Cooking* (Jonathan Cape, 1992)

Fennel and Watercress Salad © Jo Rodgers, Oxfam

Red Cabbage Coleslaw © Margaret Costa, *Four Seasons Cookery Book* (Grub Street, 1996)

Michael Barry's Coleslaw © Michael Barry, *Oxfam Vegetarian Cookbook* (Ebury Press, 1992)

Tarator Sauce © Jane Grigson *The Fish Book* (Penguin Books Ltd, 1994)

Flambéed Bananas with Kumquat Marmalade Sauce © Sophie Grigson

Baked Figs with Mascarpone and Walnuts © Nigel Slater 1993, 1994, 1995, *Real Good Food* (reprinted by permission of Fourth Estate Ltd)

Brunne © Oxfam Wereldwinkels/Magasins du Monde (Oxfam in Belgium)

Sweet Potato Pie © Jane Grigson, *The Vegetable Book* (Penguin Books Ltd, 1996)

Pears Baked with Honey © Brian Turner

Praline Chocolate Terrine © Jo Rodgers, Oxfam

Chocolate Chip Ice Cream © Anton Mosimann

Pecan Nut Torte © Rose Elliot

Bolivian Banana Surprise © Valentina Harris

Chocolate Cake © Michael Barry

Chocolate Prune and Almond Cake © Nigel Slater 1993, 1994, 1995, *Real Good Food* (reprinted by permission of Fourth Estate Ltd)

Gingerbread Cake © Gary Rhodes, *Rhodes Around Britain* (BBC Worldwide, 1994)

Christmas Cake © Paul and Jeanne Rankin

Swahili Buns by Janet McCrae, *Recipes from Around the World* © Oxfam, 1983

Date and Walnut Bread © Margaret Costa, *Four Seasons Cookery Book* (Grub Street, 1996)

Tchai © Oxfam Wereldwinkels/Magasins du Monde (Oxfam in Belgium)

Milk and Almond Drink © Madhur Jaffrey, *Eastern Vegetarian Cooking* (Jonathan Cape, 1992)

Oxfam have made every effort to trace the copyright holders for specific recipes. If they have inadvertently overlooked someone, they will be pleased to make the necessary arrangements at the first opportunity.

Index